Summary of the Walks

Walk number	Starting place	Grid ref of start OS sheet 124	Length of walk (miles)	Grade (see below)	Average time to allow for walk	Remarks
1	Ganllwyd	727243	3	Easy	2hrs	Woodlands, waterfall, old gold mining area on open hillside
2	nr Ganllwyd	735263	3½	Easy	2hrs	Wooded river valley, waterfalls
3	Llanfachreth	756225	4½	Easy	3hrs	Open countryside, extensive views
4	Bontddu	678189	3½	Easy	2½ hrs	RSPB woodland reserve
5	nr Llanelltyd	707196	4	Moderate	3hrs	Woodlands, lake, extensive views
6	Llanelltyd	719193	5	Moderate	3hrs	Woodlands, extensive views
7	nr Llanfachreth	746212	4	Easy	2hrs	Open hillside, extensive views, lake
8	Penmaenpool	696185	5	Moderate	2½hrs	Some woodlands but mainly open countryside, disused railway path beside estuary
9	nr Dolgellau	718172	3½	Easy	2hrs	Quiet country lane, extensive views
10	Dolgellau	731178	4	Moderate	3hrs	River valley, woodlands, open fields, extensive views
11	nr Brithdir	761181	2½	Easy	1½hrs	Riverside walk in a ravine
12	Cregennen Lakes	658142	5½	Easy	3hrs	Lakes, open countryside, wooded river valley
13	Ty Nant car park	698152	4	Moderate	2½hrs	Woods, moorland, lake, long views
14	Ty Nant car park	698152	4½	Moderate/ Energetic	4hrs	Moorland, mountain lake, dramatic scenery and views
15	Minffordd car park	732115	7-8	Energetic	5½-7hrs	Mountain walking, lake, spectacular views. Full day and fine weather needed.

Walk grading - No rewarding walk in this beautiful undulating area can be *completely* level.

Easy Any uphill sections are short and not steep.

Moderate Involves some uphill walking, but not for long, and easily managed by a reasonably fit person

Energetic Some long uphill sections, sometimes with steep parts and rocky underfoot but, at a moderate pace, within the capabilities of a reasonably fit person.

KITTIWAKE

LOCAL WALKS AROUND DOLGELLAU

GEOFF ELLIOTT

LOCAL AUTHOR

Fifteen circular self-guided walks suitable for all abilities

Introduction

DOLGELLAU, at the head of the magnificent Mawddach Estuary, is an ideal centre for exploring the whole of the southern half of the Snowdonia National Park. All of the walks in this book are located close to Dolgellau, with their starting points no more than a 15 minute drive away from the town by car, and all are in scenery that is remarkably varied and interesting. There are paths on high ridges, in open moorland and nature reserves, along rivers, lakes or the estuary, near waterfalls, following old mining tracks and among moss-cushioned boulders in woodlands of oak, beech, ash and birch.

Any of these walks can be undertaken by a reasonably fit person, with **Walk 15**, if the whole route is followed, being the most challenging. Walking boots or strong shoes are recommended for all of them, and *please* keep in mind that this is sheep farming country – dogs must be kept on a lead at all times (or left behind).

The location of each walk is shown on the back cover and a summary of the key characteristics of each is given opposite. An estimated time is also given, but for those who enjoy fine views, and are likely to linger over them, it is best to allow longer. The scenery is far too good to hurry through.

Each walk has a map and description which enables it to be followed without further help, but always take account of the weather, and dress accordingly, especially if you are exploring the higher routes. Also, take time to explore the town of Dolgellau – the Civic Society has published an excellent illustrated Town Trail leaflet to guide you, and this is available from the Tourist Information Centre.

About the author, Geoff Elliott ...

Geoff Elliott's strong feelings for the old county of Merionnydd developed in his twenties. Born and educated in Cardiff, he worked at the Government's Welsh Office where his duties enabled him to travel throughout Wales. Always a very keen walker, it was clear that Merionnydd (as was) had a greater variety of beautiful natural landscapes than any other county in Wales. After taking early retirement he came to live in the area he finds so appealing, making it possible to explore it more deeply, and introduce it to others. He regularly leads walks for The Ramblers' Association, is an active member of the Snowdonia National Park Society, and a voluntary National Park warden.

WALK 1
GANLLWYD – DOLMELYNLLYN

DESCRIPTION A 3 mile walk with only moderate ascents, through beautiful woodlands and visiting a spectacular waterfall. It passes the site of former gold mining operations and gives extensive views over the Coed-y-Brenin Forest. Allow 2 hours.
START Car park at Ganllwyd. SH 727243.
DIRECTIONS From Dolgellau take the A470 north-west towards Betws-y-Coed. After 5 miles, just after entering the village of Ganllwyd, the car park is on the RIGHT.

1 Leave the car park close by the National Trust information board and cross the road. Go a short distance LEFT and then turn RIGHT up a narrow surfaced road alongside the village hall, going through a road gate. *The Afon Gamlan is on the left, tumbling over boulders and rocks.* Within about 200 yards, where the road forks, go LEFT, continuing uphill. After about the same distance the road curves to the right. Leave it for a path straight ahead, to reach a waymark post which is visible about 20 yards away. At the post turn LEFT through the oak trees and moss covered boulders along a path towards the river. After 50 yards there is another waymark post indicating the path down to the river and a footbridge. Ignore this and instead continue straight ahead to a stone tablet close to a fence. *The tablet contains lines from a poem by Thomas Grey and is relatively new. The original inscription can just be made out on the stone to the left of the new tablet.* Go down to the footbridge, cross the river *(look out for heron and dippers)* and turn RIGHT along the rough path to view the falls. *Their name, Rhaeadr Ddu (the Black Falls) derives from the dark rocks over which the Gamlan plunges into two slightly separated high falls.* Follow the rough path to above the upper fall and carry on for about another 50 yards to a waymark post. As indicated, go LEFT into the wood along a narrow path. When a wall is reached go LEFT continuing on the same path, which runs roughly parallel to the wall on the right. *Look out for deer in this beautiful wood.*

2 Within about 300 yards a waymark post and ladder stile are reached. *Ignore the signed post* and turn RIGHT to cross the stile over the wall. Then turn LEFT along a wide but generally slightly overgrown track. Eventually, at conifer trees, a rough surfaced forest road is reached. Go straight across and along a wide track to another waymark post 40 yards ahead. Follow half-LEFT in the direction indicated, along the same wide track in the wood. *An old partly collapsed wall is reached, many of its stones covered in thick moss – on the other side of this is a stream rushing down from the crags ahead – Y Garn.* Keep along this track to reach another waymark post close to a wide forest road. Stay on the track, as indicated, going straight ahead to a new stile in the wall on the left, about 40 yards further on.

3 Step over this interestingly designed stile and cross the footbridge. *The buildings ahead on the open hillside are all relics of the period 1862 to 1914, when gold was being sought here. This was the Cefn Coch mine, the third richest in the Meirionnydd gold belt, which stretched along the north side of the Mawddach Estuary, from near Barmouth to close to Llanelltyd, and then roughly north almost to Trawsfynydd. Details of the buildings are in the National Trust booklet 'Dolmelynllyn', available at the car park.* Go half-RIGHT along the laid stone pathway over boggy ground and up through the small boulders to the waymark post at the wide track ahead. Go LEFT up to the buildings. *Nearby are the settling ponds, parts of the tramway, and the barracks where some of the miners lived. To the east there are fine views across the Coed y Brenin Forest to Rhobell Fawr and the Arenig Mountains. To the west is the escarpment shouldering the north-east side of Y Garn.* Carry on along the wide track, passing to the right of the ruins of the barracks, and gradually getting closer to the stone wall on the left. Soon a ladder stile over the wall is reached: cross the wall and follow the way-

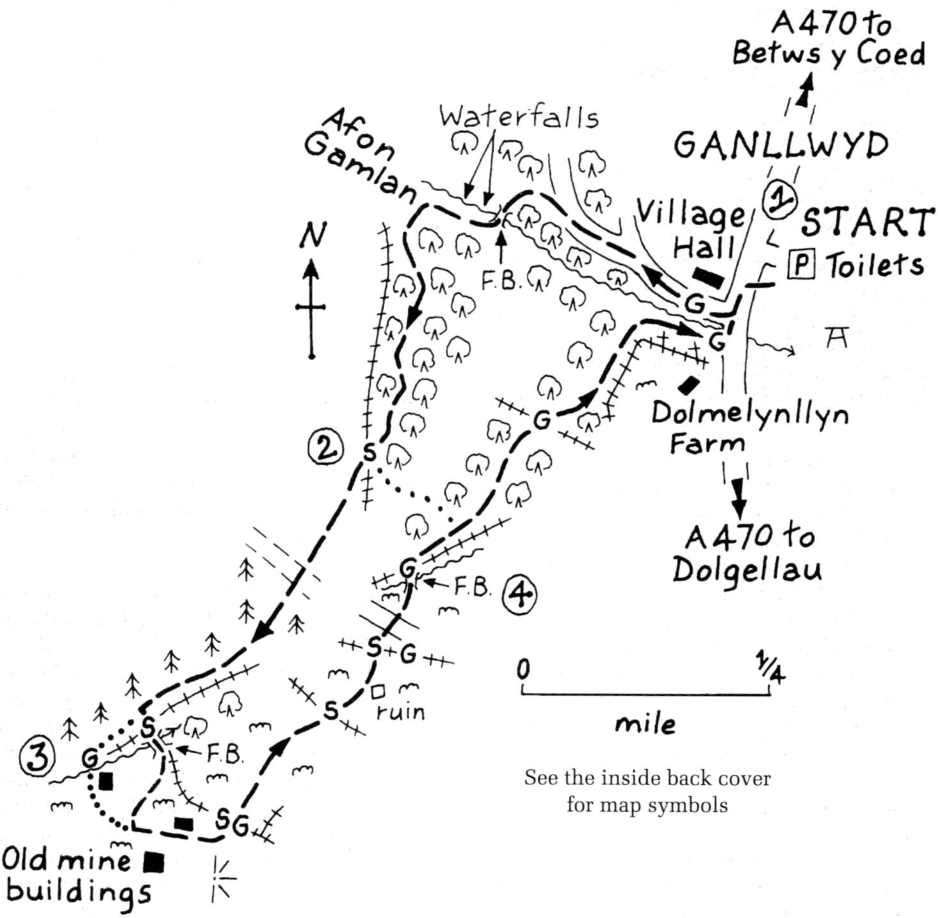

See the inside back cover for map symbols

marked path down through the bracken until another ladder stile over the next wall is reached. Cross this, and make for the small ruined building half-RIGHT ahead. Pass to the left of the building and proceed to a gate seen in the fence 75 yards ahead. Cross the fence by the stile at the side of the gate and go straight across the surfaced road, down to the footbridge and gate 100 yards ahead.

4 Go through the gate and turn RIGHT, taking the path with a wall on the right into the wood. Keep straight on at the next waymark continuing through the wood until, near the edge of the wood, a fence and a low sign post are reached. Go through the gate in the fence and down to a stone wall. Go LEFT along the wall. Soon after the wall goes sharply right, go through the gap in the fence ahead. *The Afon Gamlan is now nearby on the left.* Carry on to the wall ahead, going through a gap at the right-hand end of it and out through a gate onto the main road. The car park is 100 yards to the left.

WALK 2
COED Y BRENIN AND THE AFON MAWDDACH

DESCRIPTION An easy 3½ mile walk through mixed woodland, in a beautiful deep narrow valley seldom far from the sound of the Afon Mawddach, as it tumbles along its rocky bed. Two waterfalls and the site of one of the area's principal former gold mines are visited. Allow 2 hours.
START At a forest picnic site about 6 miles north of Dolgellau. SH 735263

DIRECTIONS Take the A470 north-west from Dolgellau in the direction of Betws y Coed. After about 5 miles the village of Ganllwyd is reached. Go through the village to the far (northern) end and, close to the traffic speed derestriction signs, turn RIGHT along a minor road. Cross the bridge over the river and go RIGHT. Park at the forest picnic site 'Tyddyn Glwladys', just over a mile further along this road.

1 Leave the picnic area alongside the Afon Mawddach and go RIGHT along the road and on to a roughly surfaced forest track. Go through a gate and continue ahead until the house *Ferndale* is reached. Pass by the road barrier to the left of the property and carry on along the road. *The derelict remains of buildings hereabouts amongst the trees are ruins from past mining activities, mainly lead and gold.* Soon after the road and river bend to the left, the first of the two waterfalls can be seen through the trees across to the right. *This is the Rhaeadr Mawddach, situated just up the river from where another river, the Afon Cain, joins the Mawddach.* Continue along the road, which goes further left and then swings right to a bridge over the Afon Cain.

2 *At the bridge the second falls – Pystyll Cain – can be seen higher up the ravine to the left.* At the far end of the bridge there is a rough narrow track to the LEFT which goes closer to the falls, and from which their full height can be seen. *This is a beautiful ravine at any time, but a visit after heavy rainfall will be especially memorable.* Return to the bridge and turn LEFT to continue along the forest road. *A short distance along to the right are the remains of the buildings associated with the Gwynfynydd gold mine where gold was first found in 1864. There was a large processing mill here but it was destroyed by fire in 1935. An information board at the site gives more details.* Continue along the road, now rising and curving to the left. Near the top of the slope *Rhaeadr Mawddach* can be seen below on the right. *The difference between the Welsh words used to name these waterfalls will now be clear: 'pistyll' where the fall, on the Cain, is narrow and spout-like; 'rhaeadr' where the fall, on the Mawddach, is much wider.* In another 150 yards there is a stone bridge across the Afon Mawddach.

3 Cross the bridge and follow the road around to the right and uphill. Where it levels out, and at a white-top post numbered 19, go RIGHT along another forest road. *The rivers are now well below on the right and soon, where the trees have been cleared, both waterfalls can be seen.* Carry on along the road and when it forks, at a white-top post numbered 20, go ahead and slightly to the RIGHT. Continue with the Mawddach generally close and below on the right, until after about one mile a wide and high footbridge across the river is reached. There is another white-top post here, numbered 51.

4 Cross the footbridge and go up to the surfaced minor road. Go RIGHT to return to the picnic site.

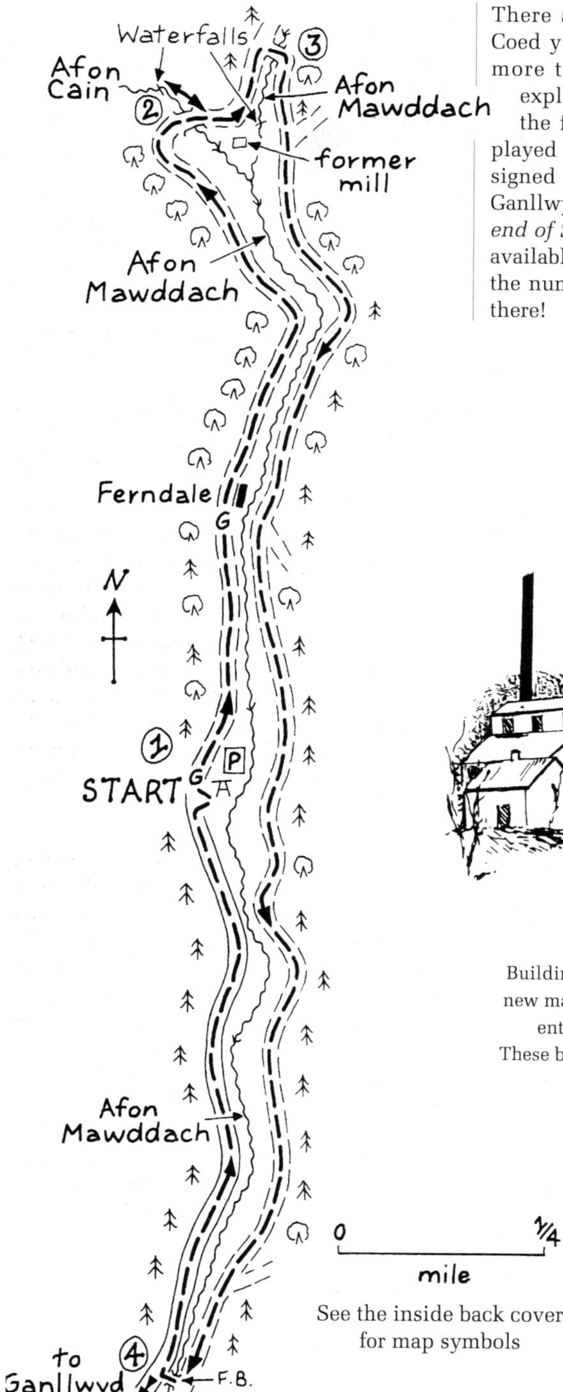

There are other attractive river valleys in Coed y Brenin (the King's Forest) and many more tracks and footpaths which can be explored. Information about the history of the forest, its mines and wildlife, is displayed at the Forest Visitor Centre which is signed off the A470 about 2 miles north of Ganllwyd. It is *open daily from Easter to the end of September*, and light refreshments are available. Well worth visiting: the mystery of the numbered white-top posts can be solved there!

Buildings at the Gwynfynydd gold mine, where new machinery was installed during a revival of enthusiasm for Welsh gold in the 1930s. These buildings were almost totally destroyed by fire in February 1935.

See the inside back cover for map symbols

WALK 3
LLANFACHRETH

DESCRIPTION An easy 4½ mile walk crossing varied terrain but mainly in open, very quiet and beautiful countryside with extensive views. Allow 3 hours.

START Parking area alongside Llanfachreth Village School. SH 756225. Toilets are available on the village side of the school.

DIRECTIONS Go north out of Dolgellau town centre and across the Afon Wnion bridge. Turn RIGHT in front of the Council Offices. After ⅓ mile turn LEFT along the minor road signed 'Precipice Walk' and 'Llanfachreth'. After 2 miles go past the car park for the Precipice Walk (see Walk 7) and continue straight on to Llanfachreth. At the village turn RIGHT to go past the church and reach the school. The parking area is on the left, just beyond the school.

1 Leave the parking area and turn RIGHT along the road, passing in front of the school. Turn RIGHT again at the side of the school, taking the signed path. Look for a gate ahead and go through it and along a wide grassy track with a fence on the left. Continue up this track until the fence on the left ends at a corner. Carry on ahead parallel to a low wall on the right, below which is a vehicular track. IGNORE the footpath sign half-right, and go ahead and across the track where it curves to the left, and ahead into the trees to reach a gate into a conifer wood.

2 Go through the gate and follow the wide path to reach another gate slightly to the right. Go through this gate and half-LEFT into an open field and along a faint track roughly parallel to the wall and fence on the left. At the end of the field go through another gate at a shallow stream crossing. Carry on ahead along the track, with the stream on the left. The path soon leaves the stream and rises gently into open ground. Then follow it to the left, to be walking parallel to, but slightly away from, an old partly broken wall on the left. *On the right there are some fine views of the foothills of Rhobell Fawr.* The path drops down to go through the wall. Keep on ahead, ignoring the misleading waymark on a tree, to go through the gap in another stone wall. Carry on, keeping close to the fence and wall on the left, to reach a waymarked gate.

3 Go through the gate and follow the faint track through the rock outcrops, keeping roughly parallel to the fence on the right. Cross a small stream and continue along the rising track which now veers slightly left, away from the wall on the right, and passes to the right of some large rocky outcrops ahead. This grassy track soon joins a rough surfaced road which comes in from below on the right. Carry on ahead along this road. *There are extensive views back to Cadair Idris and the Dyfi Forest.* Go through a gate and over the pass, Bwlch Goriwared. *Once through the pass there are fine views ahead across Coed y Brenin and beyond.* Go through another gate, and the track drops down to join a forest road. Turn LEFT and go slightly uphill for about 100 yards to a white-top post (number 45) on the left. Go LEFT here, following the narrow waymarked path up through the young trees to reach, at the top, a stone wall and gate.

4 Go through the gate into an open area of heather and moorland grass. Carry on straight ahead along a path at the bottom of a sloping heather-covered bank on the right. Continue along this narrow path for about 200 yards to where it divides at a small heap of stones. Go half-LEFT through the heather along another narrow path, soon crossing a very small stream, and then continuing along a flat corridor of grassland just to the left of a prominent, heather-covered, rocky knoll. At the far end of the knoll, carry on in the same direction, going gently uphill, and again following just to the left of another sloping, heather-covered, rocky bank. The path soon becomes clearer again. Follow it through the heather to the top of the rise. *Here there are extensive views to the right (west) across Coed y Brenin to the Rhinogydd, south-west to Y Garn, and straight ahead to Foel Offrwm (in the foreground) and Cadair Idris beyond.*

5 At the wall ahead go through the gap, and immediately drop down half-RIGHT to the bottom of the small valley. Turn LEFT along the grassy track towards a wall ahead. At the wall go half-RIGHT alongside it. *Llyn Cynwch and the Precipice Walk (see Walk 7) are now visible ahead with, just a little further to the right, Bryniau Glo (see Walk 6) prominent on the far side of the Mawddach Valley.* Continue on down along the track near the wall. *Even more extensive views open up, this time to the left, to the Arans.* The track passes the ruins of a former farmhouse on the left, and then soon reaches a surfaced road alongside an occupied property, *Tyn y Mynydd.* Follow the road down, through two gates, to Llanfachreth. At the crossroads turn LEFT to the school and the parking area.

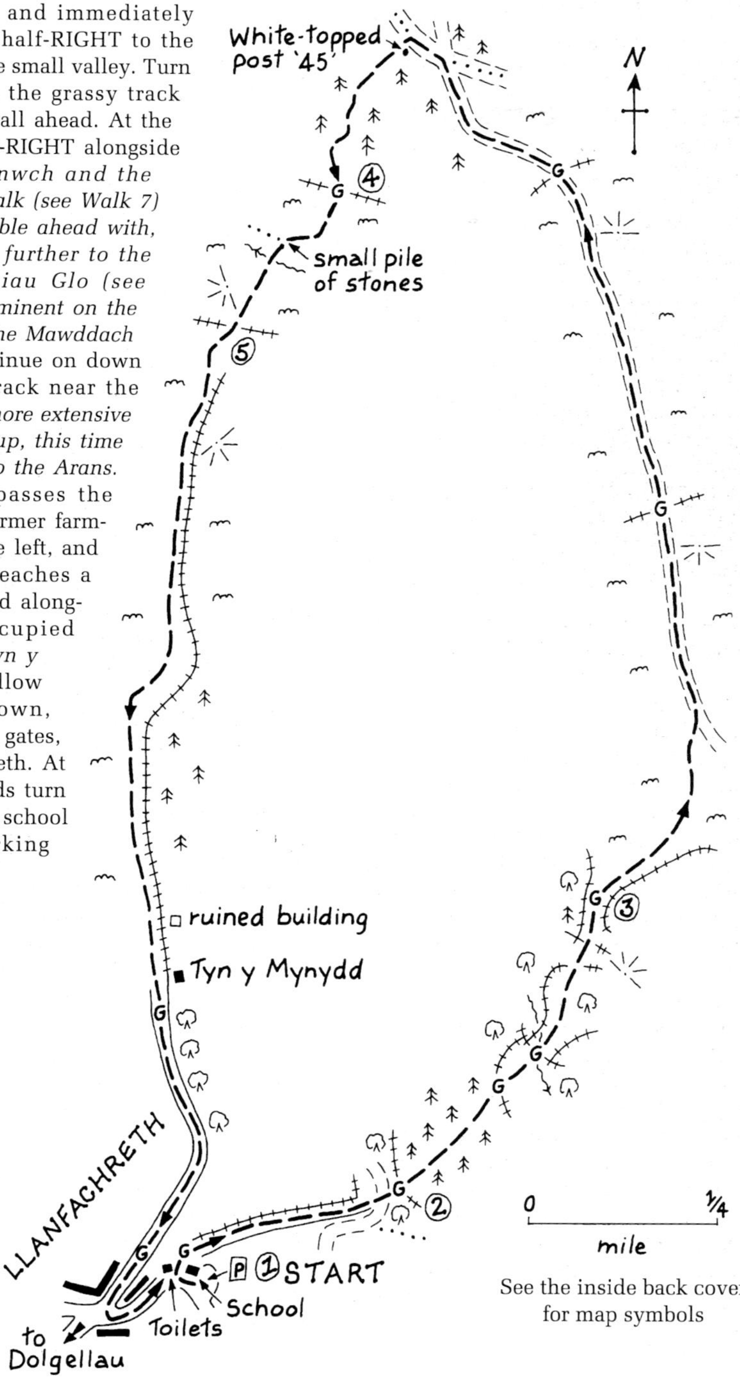

See the inside back cover for map symbols

WALK 4
COED GARTH GELL RESERVE

DESCRIPTION An easy 3½ mile walk, mainly in the beautiful deciduous woodlands of an RSPB reserve, with spectacular views of the Afon Mawddach estuary. Buzzards, ravens, dippers and wagtails are seen all year, and there are many visiting summer birds. The walk is on the gold-mining belt which runs along the north side of the Mawddach estuary: there are interesting industrial remains. Allow 2½ hours.

START National Park car park and picnic site at Fiddler's Elbow, a short distance east of Bontddu, on the A496 about 5 miles from Dolgellau. SH 678189.

DIRECTIONS From Dolgellau go north-west along the A470 towards Betws-y-Coed. After 2 miles, at Llanelltyd, turn LEFT along the A496 towards Barmouth. The lay-by car park and picnic area is at a National Park sign about 3 miles along on the right, just before Bontddu village.

1 From the car park go up the footpath-signed wide driveway amongst the trees. Stay on this lane, going very sharp RIGHT where it makes a turn at the top of the hill. The lane climbs again but soon levels out. Go through the gate ahead into the grounds of a modern dwelling, *Penygribin*. It is a private drive, but a public right of way. Keep on the driveway towards the house door, then go LEFT under an archway at the end of the building. Keep left across the garden grass and go LEFT along the narrow track waymarked on a tree ahead. Go over a stile in the fence ahead and continue along the path through the trees. Soon cross another stile and carry on until a wall and fence are reached. Go straight ahead along the narrow path between the wall and the fence. Continue close to the wall until another wall across the path is reached. Go through the gap in it and carry on ahead keeping close to another, higher, stone wall on the right. The remains of an old stone building are reached on the right, together with a low *'visitor route'* sign.

2 *The path now enters the Coed Garth-gell Reserve, owned by the RSPB.* Continue straight ahead along the path indicated by the sign. The path winds through woodland, passing to the right of the ruins of an old cottage, and continues downhill to join a wide track. Go RIGHT, downhill to an RSPB information board. Go LEFT along the path indicated by the *visitor route* sign, alongside a fence on the right. The path soon goes through an old gateway and enters Cwm Mynach, the monks' valley. *The river below on the right is Afon Cwm-mynach, and the track is a former tramway, used in the last century in connection with mining operations. Before that it might well also have been one of the routes used by the monks of Cymer Abbey, just north of Dolgellau, who owned land here and whose advanced farming practices would have encouraged tree clearance and sheep breeding in the upper, broader sections of this valley. Whatever its history it is a beautiful path to walk now.* After about ⅓ mile the site of a former mill is reached. *The interesting six round structures low down near the river are the foundations of buddles, used in the process of separating out the metal ores.*

3 Carry on along the track up the valley to reach the old smithy. Go straight head passing to the right of the building. *The path now becomes more open, allowing views of the hills across the valley on the right.* Keep on the path as it curves LEFT and away from the river. It soon curves around to the RIGHT and reaches a gate and ladder stile over a wall. Ignore the *visitor route* to the left and go over the ladder stile and along the wide track leading ahead from the gate. It curves slightly right and passes to the right of the top of a small knoll ahead, climbing slightly. After passing the knoll and its few trees, the broad path is in an open area *giving fine views ahead and across to the other side of Cwm Mynach.* Keep on this path up to a gate in the wall ahead. DO NOT GO THROUGH, but turn sharp LEFT keeping in the same field, and with the wall on the right.

Continue along to a gap in the wall and turn LEFT again, keeping parallel to the wall, which later becomes a fence, on the right. At the end of the field, and a little way down the wall from the corner, is a ladder stile alongside a gate.

4 Go over the stile and enter the reserve again. *The route, until the last section in the open field, was roughly north. Now it heads south and at the stile there is a good view directly ahead of Penygadair, at 2928 feet the highest point of the Cadair Idris range, and slightly to its right, of Cyfrwy, a little lower at 2646 feet. They are nearly 5 miles away across the Mawddach Valley (Walk 14 passes close to them).* Carry on along the path. It eventually drops down through a gap in a low stone wall. Continue ahead along the winding path through the trees, passing a bench. *It is on this section that there are the finest views, to the left and slightly back, of the hills on the other side of Cwm Mynach, reaching to the summit of Y Garn.* Keep ahead on the obvious path, through another old wall, and reaching a substantial wall with a *visitor route* sign indicating to go through the gap in it. There is another bench here. *Just beyond are fine views of the whole of the Cadair Idris range and, below, of the hamlet of Penmaenpool (Walk 8) on the other side of the Afon Mawddach, but linked to this side by the wooden toll bridge.* Continue along and go through yet another gap. When past a gorse and heather covered knoll ahead, *even more spectacular views open up: the rough tops of Pared y Cefn-hir (Walk 12) further down the Mawddach, and right on to the mouth of the estuary at Barmouth. There is a conveniently placed bench a little ahead, from which the views extend to the Aran Mountains in the extreme east and around to the sea in the west.* The path continues down into the trees.

5 At the bottom of the dell another *visitor route* sign indicates a path to the left. *Do not take this* but go RIGHT along a broad path towards a stone wall. Continue ahead alongside the wall to a gate ahead. Go through and continue ahead with a wall on the left. Soon there is a gate in this wall: carry on past it until another similar gate is reached. Go through this gate out on to the lane and turn RIGHT, to the car park.

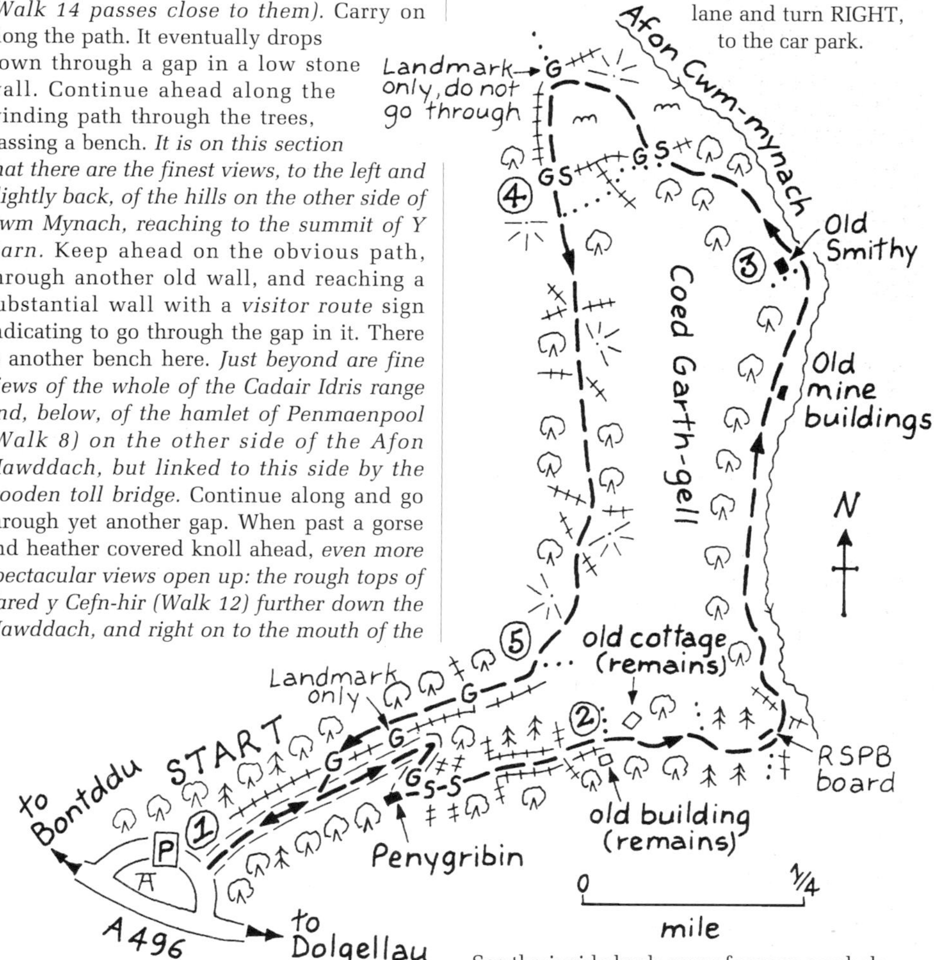

See the inside back cover for map symbols

WALK 5
NEW PRECIPICE WALK

DESCRIPTION A moderate 4 mile walk with outstanding views from an old industrial tramway 800 feet above the Mawddach Estuary. The path climbs steadily and fairly steeply from the start, but with a rest possible at an attractive lake set in the hills. After the tramway the path drops through both deciduous and evergreen trees, with a short section following the course of an old leat (water course), constructed over 100 years ago. Allow 3 hours.

START Park at an old road lay-by on the A496. SH 707196.

DIRECTIONS From Dolgellau go north-west along the A470 towards Betws-y-coed. After 2 miles, at Llanelltyd, turn LEFT along the A496 towards Barmouth. Look for the traffic derestriction signs about ½ mile along this road. Just beyond them the road bends to the left and then to the right. *Immediately after* the bend to the right, SLOW DOWN and look for the footpath sign on the right hand side, at an old road lay-by now used for parking. Turn RIGHT into this.

1 Walk along the parking area to almost the far (western) end of the still surfaced old road. Go into the wood through a gap where the stone embankment ends at a large boulder, not far from a stream. Almost immediately the path divides. Do NOT continue straight ahead parallel to the stream on the left, but go half-RIGHT uphill soon to be walking parallel to the lay-by below on the right. The path reaches a low stone wall where it curves left and then left again at a garden gate. Keep along this path uphill, soon going sharp right and passing relics of former mining operations on the left. The path again goes left at another stone wall, *and very soon a better view is obtained, below on the left, of the industrial ruins. At these ruins the main path is seen going straight ahead.* However, **look for, and take**, a less distinct path half-RIGHT going more steeply uphill and running parallel to the stone wall over on the right. Proceed along this path up to the conifer plantation ahead. *As the path approaches the evergreen trees there is a fine view back down the Mawddach Estuary to the railway bridge at Barmouth.*

2 Go into the forest plantation along the broad path directly ahead and uphill. Soon after it levels out, Llyn Tan-y-graig is seen through the trees as a crossing of paths is reached. (*For a closer look at the lake, and the fine views from it over Dolgellau, go straight ahead and over the ladder stile at the edge of the wood. Return over the stile and back to this crossing.)* Turn LEFT (right if you have been to the lake) following the waymarked path uphill through more trees. After levelling out, the path crosses a small stream and again goes uphill through trees. Keep along this main path and, when it curves to the left and narrows, go through a less dense area of pine trees, with steeply sloping ground down to the left. *There are soon glimpses of the panoramic views to come.* The path, still cushioned by old brown pine needles, eventually crosses another small stream just before a ladder stile in the wall ahead.

3 Go over the stile and turn LEFT alongside the wall. Pass to the right of the ruined house ahead and cross the footbridge over the stream. Carry on ahead, parallel to the wall and passing another ruined building. After about another 100 yards the path leaves the wall on the left and goes uphill to a gap in the wall ahead. DO NOT go up the much steeper path going further to the right, which is part of an old tramway incline. *This is the end of climbing and the start of the magnificent views from the 'precipice' along the side of Foel Ispri. Ahead, westwards, is the beautiful Mawddach Estuary, completely covered at high tide, and at other times displaying winding silver ribbons reaching to the sea at Barmouth. To the south is the whole length of the Cadair Idris ridge and the undulating landscape between it and the Mawddach. The hamlet below, at the end of the wooden bridge, is Penmaenpool (see Walk 8). Far to*

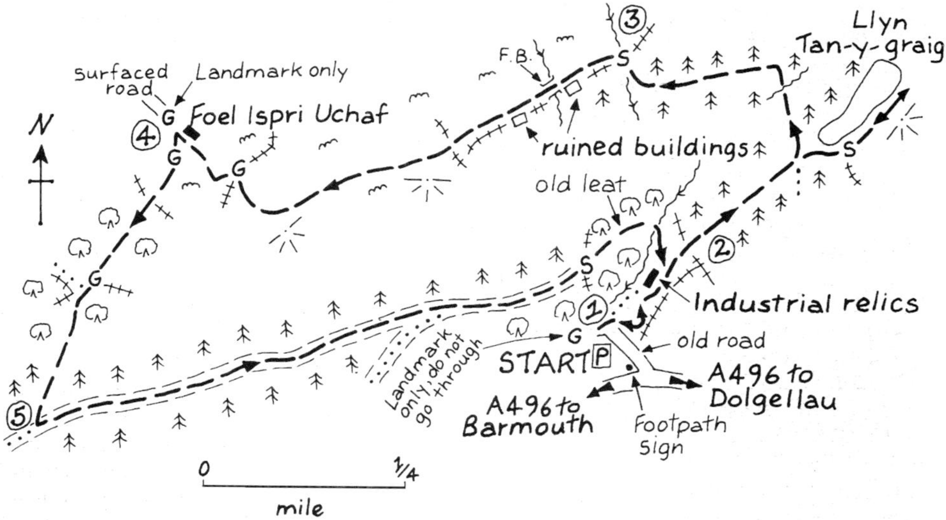

See the inside back cover for map symbols

the east are the Aran Mountains. The path now follows an old level tramway used in the last half of the nineteenth century to transport zinc and lead ore to a mill in Cwm-mynach (see Walk 4). Carry on along the tramway, eventually going through a swing gate and passing in front of and below an occupied house, *Foel Ispri Uchaf.*

4 Just beyond the house there is a gate at the start of a surfaced road. Do NOT go through this but turn back sharp LEFT down a wide green track to a waymarked gate. Go through and continue downhill, soon turning half-RIGHT at a waymark sign. The path reaches and goes through an old, mainly demolished, low wall. After about a further 50 yards, follow the waymarked path to the left of some gorse bushes, continuing downhill alongside young oak trees on the left. Follow the obvious path down. In the trees it curves left, then right, to reach a gate in a wall. Go through, continuing downhill to reach another waymarked post close to a wall. Go LEFT downhill following the path into the conifer trees and which eventually reaches a rough surfaced and wide forestry track.

5 Turn LEFT along the track. *Ignore the wide track which goes sharp right after ⅔ mile,* and carry on straight ahead. Where the track ends at a fence, go left a short distance along the fence and over a stile into the deciduous wood. Go through the old wall and straight ahead along the path into the wood, reaching the course of an old leat. Go RIGHT alongside this leat which soon reaches a stream. *In certain conditions the stream may have two separate courses.* Cross the stream and go sharp RIGHT along the clear path. It soon drops down through bracken in a more open area from which there are splendid views down the Estuary. The path then joins the outward route close to the industrial relics, now below on the right. Follow the path down to the lay-by.

WALK 6
AROUND BRYNIAU GLO

DESCRIPTION A moderate 5 mile walk giving dramatic near and long-distance views. The route goes through varied woodland, with one high level open section along a narrow path, where young children will need close supervision. Some uphill, but not too steep, parts. Allow about 3 hours.

START National Park car park and picnic area alongside the Afon Mawddach, close to the old road bridge south of Llanelltyd. SH 719193.

DIRECTIONS Take the A470 north-west from Dolgellau towards Betws y Coed. Just outside Dolgellau, and before crossing the river bridge to Llanelltyd, turn RIGHT (east) along the minor road signed Cymer Abbey. This road reaches the old bridge in about ⅓ mile. The car park is on the right.

1 Leave the car park via the entrance and turn RIGHT to cross the old bridge over the Afon Mawddach. *There is a fine view back from the bridge of the three peaks of Cadair Idris: from east to west – Mynydd Moel, Penygadair and Cyfrwy.* Immediately after the bridge go half-RIGHT along the signed footpath. At the end of the path, at some houses, go ahead up a surfaced lane to the main road. *St Illtud's Church is on the left. It dates originally from the 13th century and has many interesting features, including a now rare circular churchyard. There are helpful explanatory notes inside and a visit is worthwhile.* Cross the road and go up the steps ahead to reach a minor road. Turn RIGHT along it. Where it joins the road coming up from the village go LEFT for 30 yards, then RIGHT along a signed, roughly surfaced, wide track. After about ⅓ mile the track divides. Keep RIGHT and carry on to a stile over a fence.

2 Cross the stile and go ahead along a narrow path with a fence on the left. This is the start of the section where young children need to be closely supervised. The river below is the Afon Mawddach. *There are fine views up the valley with the hill Rhobell Fawr dominating in the distance, half-right ahead. Across the valley, to the right, the path of the Precipice Walk (Walk 7) can be seen high up on Foel Cynwch.* Cross the ladder stile reached at the end of the trees on the left and continue along the path ahead, which is now in the open. Where it widens and curves right and left at a rocky knoll it is worth looking back down the valley towards Cadair Idris.

3 Carry on to another ladder stile over a wall. Cross it and go ahead along the path through oak trees. After about 60 yards the path curves LEFT at the edge of the trees and continues through bracken to the corner of a low stone wall on the left, to the left of a high rocky mound. After just another 10 yards, at the end of the wall, go LEFT along the narrow path through the bracken, soon with an old low wall on the right. Follow the wall on the right, and in about 50 yards reach a small rocky outcrop on the left, together with a small pile of stones. *The stones may still be holding up a wooden stake, which was an old signpost.* Go around the stones sharp LEFT, picking out the path through the bracken to reach another low stone wall in about 40 yards. Keep on ahead with the wall on the right, and at the wall corner in another 40 yards, follow the path just half-RIGHT where the wall itself turns sharp right. The path rises slightly and soon goes through gaps close together in two walls, probably enclosing old sheep pens. Carry on ahead with walls about 30 yards apart on either side. *There are extensive views northwards across the Coed y Brenin forest to the distant mountains of northern Snowdonia.* The path drops down to cross a small stream. After passing close to some rock outcrops on the left it is best to move slightly LEFT towards the wall on the left to reach a gate in about 100 yards. Go through, dropping down to cross another small stream, and carry on keeping close to the wall on the left. Where the wall goes half left, follow it. The route soon begins to level out. *A short diversion across the open* *ground on the right up to the top of the small rocky outcrops will be rewarded with magnificent views; it is the highest point on the walk.* Carry on parallel to the wall to reach a gate into a conifer wood.

4 Go through the gate and along a cushioned path of brown needles. When, in about 60 yards, it divides, go LEFT down through the dark pines. The path emerges at a forest road. Go LEFT along it and in about ½ mile reach a minor surfaced road. Go LEFT again. This valley is Cwm Wnin. *After about ¼ mile there is a signed footpath through the trees on the right. This leads to a footbridge over the Afon Wnin, and this beautiful spot is a pleasant diversion.* Returning to the road carry on along it to Llanelltyd. Just past the speed restriction signs turn RIGHT along the road used on the outward route. Near to the end of this road go LEFT down the steps to the church and the car park.

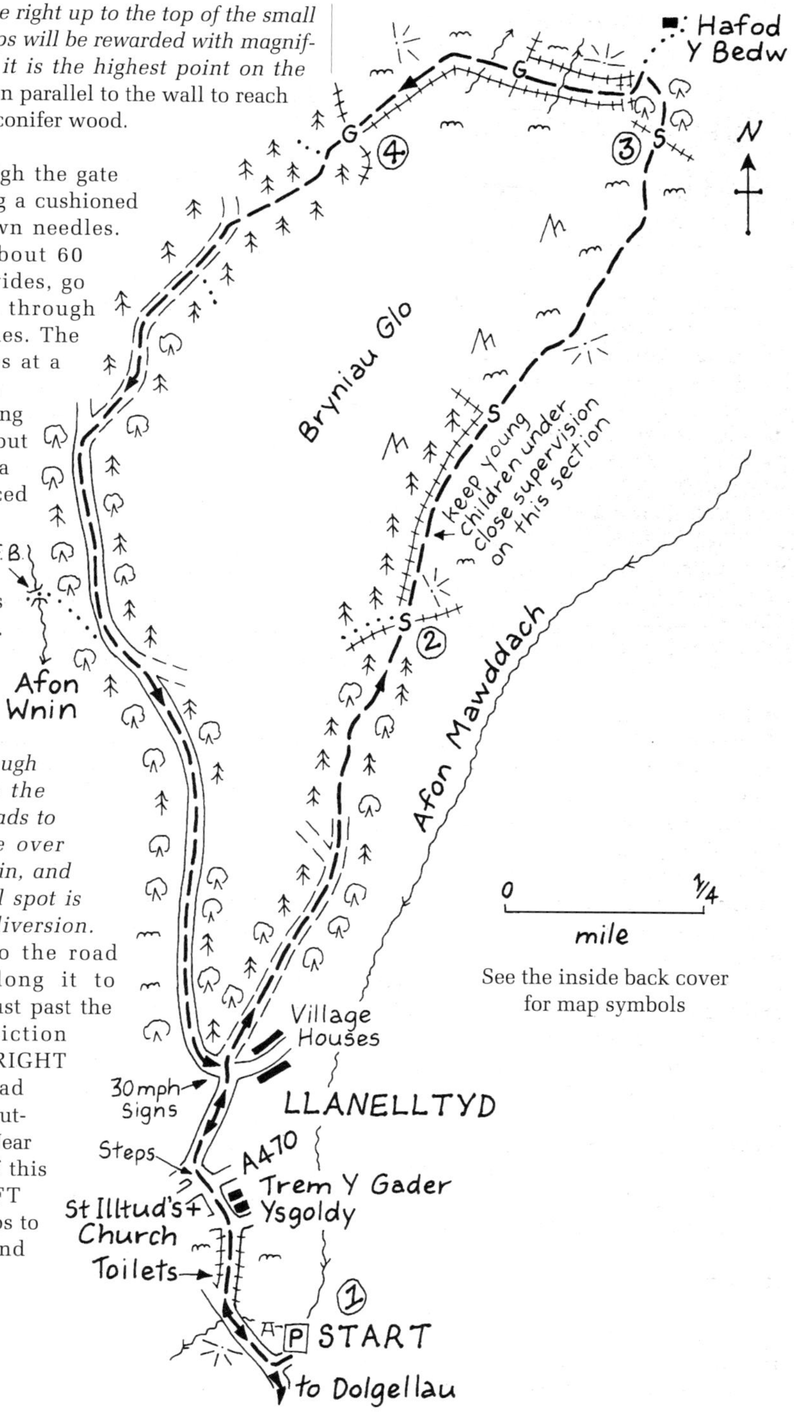

See the inside back cover for map symbols

WALK 7
PRECIPICE WALK

DESCRIPTION A very popular and easy to follow 4 mile walk, along which are a series of small informative plaques. There are outstanding views over the Mawddach valley and estuary, Coed y Brenin Forest, and the Cadair Idris range. There are no steep gradients. Allow 2 hours, although you are likely to want to stay longer.

START A National Park car park specifically for the walk will be found at the start. SH 746212.

DIRECTIONS Go north out of Dolgellau over the Afon Wnion bridge and turn RIGHT in front of the Council offices. After ⅓ mile turn LEFT along the minor road signed 'Llanfachreth' and 'Precipice Walk'. The car park is 2 miles further along on your left.

1 From the car park turn LEFT along the road signed 'Hermon', and after about 100 yards go LEFT again on a rough surfaced track into a wood. Within about 200 yards, at the end of the wood, follow the track RIGHT and, when a cottage is reached, go LEFT. *There is a view to your left here of Nannau Hall, built in 1693 and until the 1960s the home of the Vaughan family, the large landowners in this area. Most of the cottages hereabouts belonged to the estate: their often unusually high and elaborate chimneys are a feature of the estate architecture.* Climb the low ladder stile ahead and turn RIGHT. Follow this path as it curves to the left and on to climb another ladder stile. Go straight ahead to the footpath sign near the end of the wall on your right.

2 Follow the direction of the sign along the wall around to the RIGHT, go over a ladder stile and keep ahead on the clear path with the wall still on your right. *There are extensive views over the wall towards the village of Llanfachreth (see Walk 3) and its church, set below the hill Rhobell Fawr: further to the right in the far distance are the Aran mountains, the highest in Meirionnydd at 2970 feet, while sharp right, and much closer, is Foel Offrwm, topped by an Iron Age hill fort.* As the path leaves the wall and curves around to the left, *the undulating wooded slopes of the Coed y Brenin Forest (the King's Forest) are seen and, if the air is clear, some of the higher mountains of northern Snowdonia.* Continuing along the path and after climbing a ladder stile, you are soon high above the Afon Mawddach. *On the opposite side of the valley (where part of Walk 6 can be seen) are the lower slopes and upper open grassland of Y Garn. The Mawddach Estuary and the sea beyond Barmouth gradually come into view.* Climb another ladder stile and soon the whole of the Cadair Idris range and its magnificent northern escarpment are visible directly ahead. Continue along the path and, after climbing a ladder stile over a wall, Dolgellau can be seen in the valley between you and Cadair Idris. The path gradually bears left, away from the estuary, and reaches another ladder stile.

3 Climb the stile and Llyn Cynwch comes into view. Follow the path straight ahead to reach the shore at a footpath sign. Turn sharp LEFT here along the shore and continue along the tree lined path which keeps close to the lake. *At the end of the lake look back over it and to Cadair Idris far beyond; a view to cherish.* The path now rejoins the outward route and can be retraced back to the car park.

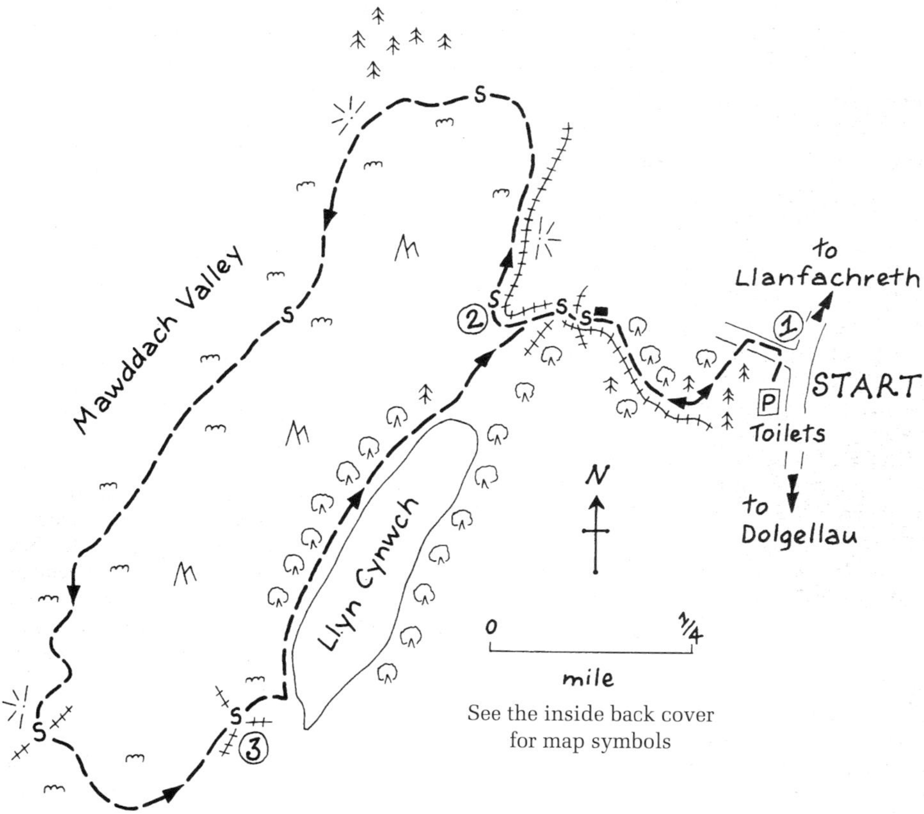

See the inside back cover for map symbols

Nannau Hall

WALK 8
THE MAWDDACH ESTUARY AT PENMAENPOOL

DESCRIPTION A 5 mile walk with some moderate uphill sections near the start, but with outstanding views of mountains and the estuary. The route passes through varied woodland and open countryside, and finishes amidst the peace of Wales' most beautiful estuary, using the track of a disused railway. Take binoculars to see the estuarial birds. Allow 2½ hours.

START At the National Park car park close to the toll bridge at Penmaenpool. SH 696185.

DIRECTIONS From Dolgellau take the A493 road to Tywyn. After about 2½ miles, just as Penmaenpool is reached, turn RIGHT at the 30 mph signs for the toll bridge road to Barmouth. About 30 yards further on turn RIGHT again into the car park.

1 Leave the car park by going past the toilet block and the RSPB Wildlife Centre, on to the narrow road in front of the hotel. Go as far as the old railway signal (about 100 yards) and take the path half LEFT up to the hotel entrance; then go sharp LEFT to the road. Turn RIGHT along the road. After 75 yards go sharp LEFT along a signed path into a wood. Continue along this winding path for about 100 yards until a gate is reached. Go through it onto a minor road. Turn LEFT along the road and when, in 200 yards, it forks, take the RIGHT fork along a roughly surfaced forestry track. Continue for about ⅓ mile until a pond is reached low down on the left, and just before the track takes a sharp bend to the left.

2 Opposite the pond take the waymarked path half RIGHT into the wood. It climbs moderately steeply. After 200 yards go over a ladder stile and continue ahead through oak trees into a flat and more open area. Look for a rough surfaced track just ahead and turn RIGHT along it. When, in about 100 yards, it

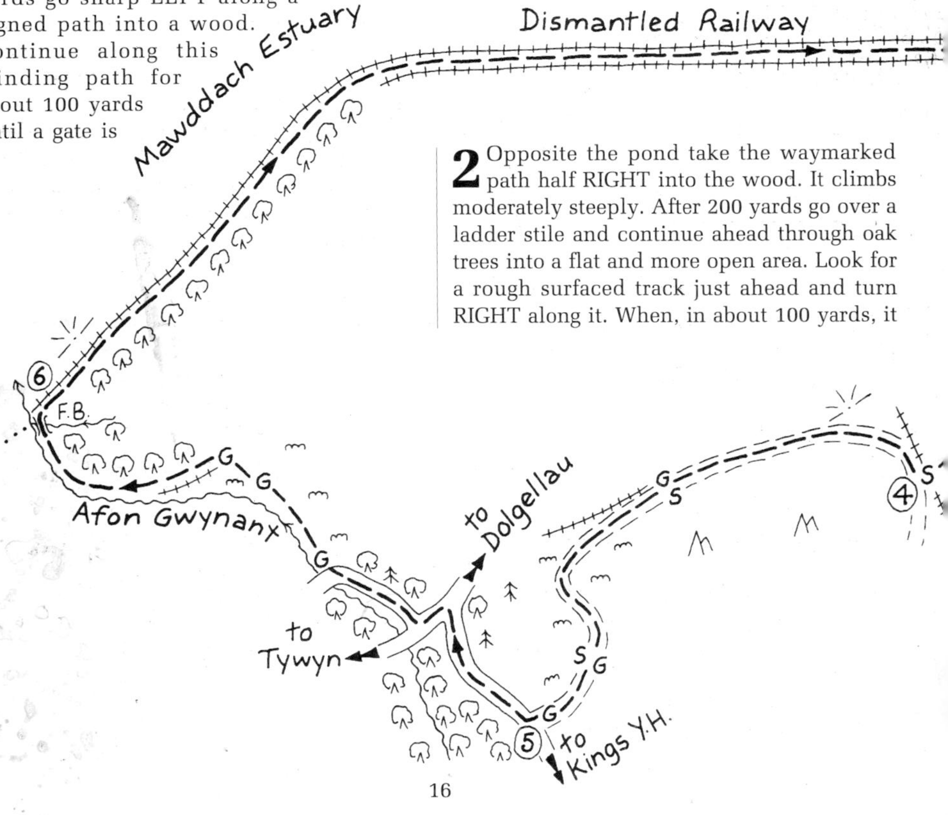

divides, go RIGHT and continue through a gap ahead in an old wall. Stay on the track, crossing two ladder stiles and then going through a gate into a farmyard. *There are fine views from this track to the Cadair Idris range far away on the left.* In the farmyard turn RIGHT and go through a gate to the right of a stone outbuilding into an open field.

3 Go LEFT and, passing close to an isolated ash tree, aim for a wooden post about 200 yards ahead at the top of the sloping field. *From near the post there are extensive views back over Dolgellau and beyond to the Aran Mountains, while to the right (south) the Cadair Idris range is again in sight.* At the post turn RIGHT along a wide track and follow this across a small shallow stream and

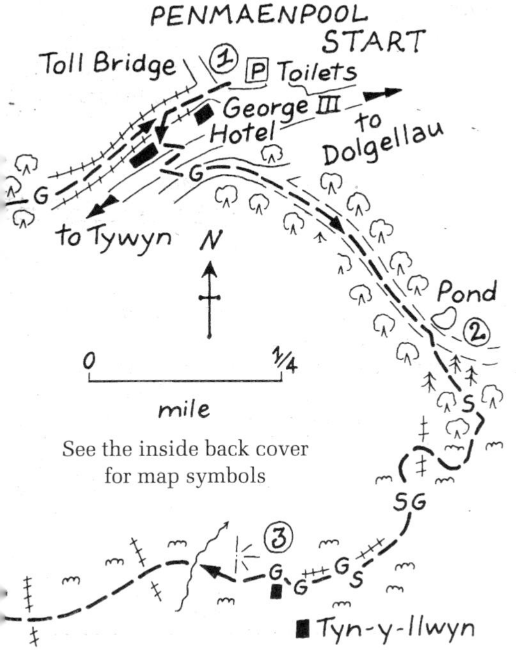

See the inside back cover for map symbols

then through a gap in an old wall into another field. Go straight ahead, keeping roughly parallel to the fence (which becomes a wall) on your left, and making for another gap in a wall about 250 yards ahead. Pass through the gap and bear slightly RIGHT keeping clear of the marshy ground on the left. When opposite the far end of the massive rock scree on your left go partly RIGHT through low gorse and up a grass track to the top of the rise. *From here there is a fine first view of the Mawddach Estuary.* Carry on half LEFT towards the wall ahead and to the ladder stile in the left corner of the field.

4 Cross the stile and go RIGHT along a rough surfaced track. *There are soon more extensive views of the estuary and Barmouth bridge and, as you continue downhill, the wooded slopes of the Gwynant valley.* Stay on this track, crossing two ladder stiles and then going through a gate onto a minor road.

5 Turn RIGHT and continue down this road to the main Dolgellau – Tywyn road. Turn LEFT but in 25 yards turn RIGHT along the narrow road signed to *Abergwynant Farm. The Afon Gwynant is now close on your left.* In about ¼ mile the road crosses the river. *Do not cross* but go straight ahead through a gate and along a rough surfaced track, keeping the river on your left. Follow the track through two more gates (the second has a wooden owl on the post). After this gate go LEFT along the track. When an open area is reached stay close to the river and take the narrow path through the small trees straight ahead *(do NOT follow the wide track going half right into the wood).* After a few yards cross a footbridge and go up onto the old railway track.

6 Turn RIGHT and follow what was once the railway track for about 1¾ miles back to Penmaenpool, and the car park.

It is flat all the way back, of course, and there are fine views over the Mawddach Estuary, with an opportunity to observe the many visiting birds (as long as you have remembered to bring along your binoculars!). The railway track which once occupied this route used to carry trains from near Barmouth to Dolgellau, but it was closed, like so many other rural lines, in the 1960s. The former signal box at Penmaenpool is now the RSPB Wildlife Centre.

WALK 9
TAL Y WAEN

DESCRIPTION This is an easy-to-follow 3½ mile walk with fine panoramic views. It can be taken by parents with children in pushchairs, as it is entirely on surfaced but very quiet roads, which for all but a short section serve merely to give access to a few nearby farms. Any length of the walk would also be suitable for wheelchair users and their helpers. As it is in varied and always interesting countryside it is also a walk, of course, for all who enjoy fine views but do not object to walking along a quiet and little-used road.

START At a minor road junction ½ mile from Dolgellau, along the road towards the Cadair Idris car park at Ty Nant. SH 718172.

DIRECTIONS The start is just under ¾ mile from the centre of Dolgellau: if you wish to park your car in the town, walk from the town centre along Cadair Road towards Tywyn. Then, near the edge of the town, take the minor road going half LEFT, signed 'Cadair Idris'. The start is ½ mile along this road where another minor road leads off to the right towards *Bryn y Gwin* farm. For those coming by car there is room at this quiet junction to park. For drivers with wheelchair-user passengers who may wish to try only a short length of this walk, follow the walk directions and park in one of the open areas alongside the road in the section with the extensive views (marked X-Y on the map). This is after the third cattle grid, but before the first gate across the road.

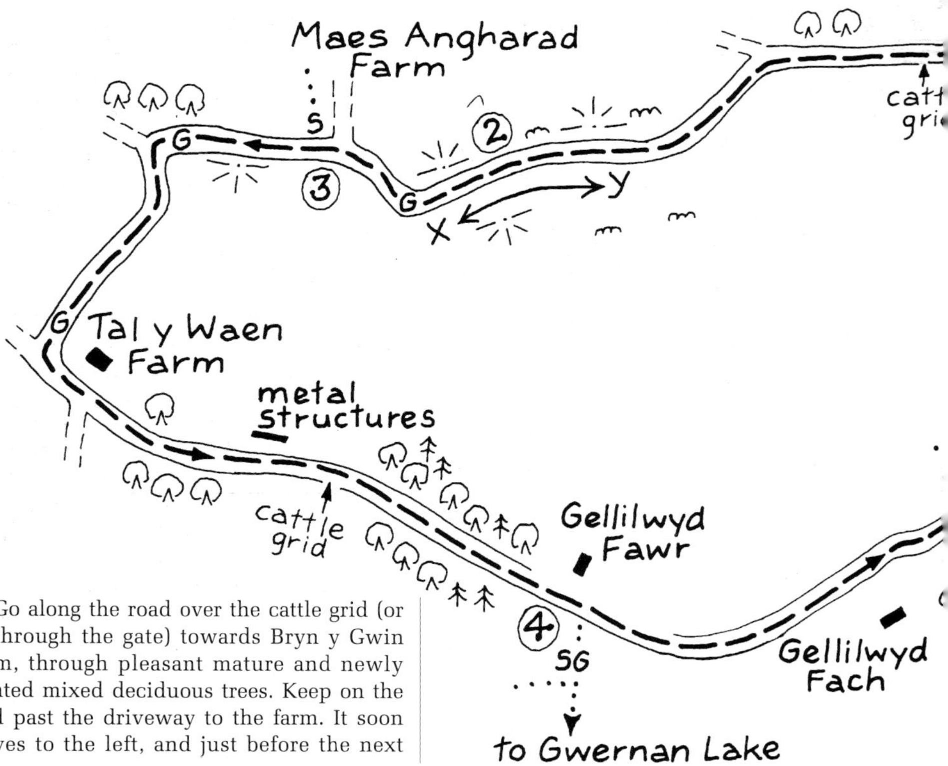

1 Go along the road over the cattle grid (or through the gate) towards Bryn y Gwin Farm, through pleasant mature and newly planted mixed deciduous trees. Keep on the road past the driveway to the farm. It soon curves to the left, and just before the next cattle grid and gate are glimpses to the right of the fine views to come. Continue along the road. There is soon another grid and beyond this, after the road goes slightly left, it enters an open area with much hawthorn, gorse and bracken. *There are clear views to the right, across to the hills on the other side of the Mawddach Estuary. Directly opposite is the route of the New Precipice Walk (see Walk 5) and it is possible to pick out, about two-thirds up the steep slope of Foel Ispri, the horizontal line of the former mineral tramway, which is now part of that walk. The higher top immediately above Foel Ispri, but set further back, is Y Garn. To the left of Ispri, and also set back, is the high ridge running south-west from the Rhinogydd mountains to Barmouth at the mouth of the Estuary.*

2 Carry on along the road. At the top of the first rise the Cadair Idris range comes into

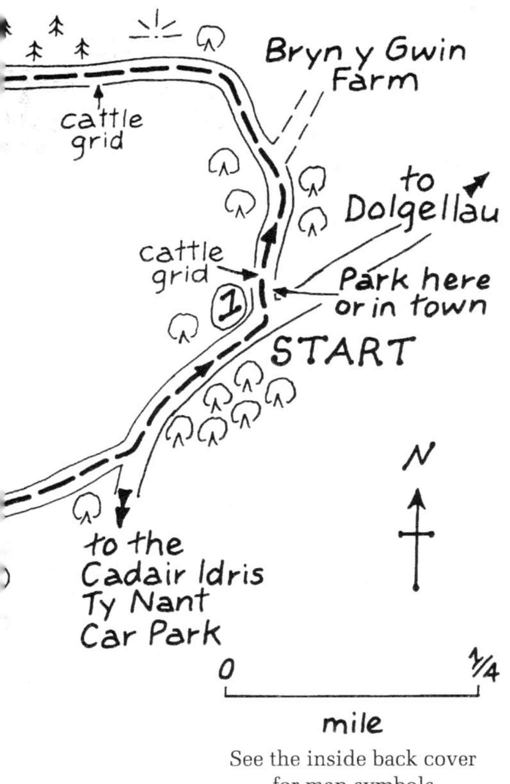

See the inside back cover for map symbols

view on the left. *The three peaks from left to right (east to west) are Mynydd Moel, Pen y Gadair (2928 feet) and Cyfrwy.* The road now dips but then quickly rises again, and at the top of this rise are the most extensive views. *To the right, looking far back (north-east) is the village of Llanelltyd, beyond which the Afon Mawddach runs in a deep, steep sided valley. This valley is the area for two other walks: Walk 6 – Bryniau Glo on the west side, and Walk 7 – Precipice Walk on the east. The mountains well beyond the far end of the valley are the Arenigs. To their right, and much nearer, is the dome-shaped Rhobell Fawr, and the long high ranges set back even further right are the Arans.* Continue along the road, which now drops, and through the gate.

3 After some bends the entrance to *Maes Angharad* farm is reached. Here the road goes sharply left, and there is a waymarked stile on the right. The road is again in an open area, with fine views to Cadair Idris on the left. Pass through a gate, soon after which the road bends left, and reach Tal y Waen Farm. Go through another gate and carry on to some birch woodland with many moss covered boulders. Just beyond the woodland, on the left, are some high old metal structures set in a small ditch alongside a walled embankment. *Trying to decide what these were can make an interesting break in the walk! (The answer is below).*

4 The next building reached further along the road is Gellilwyd Fawr *a former farmhouse with a wagon entrance, graded roofing slates, and chimneys typical of the Dolgellau area, with projecting horizontal slate slabs to help direct rainwater away from the vulnerable area at the base of the stack. Just beyond this farm the track from the ladder stile on the right leads to Gwernan Lake (Walk 13).* Continue along the road, now dropping and with occasional glimpses of parts of Dolgellau in the valley ahead. When the road joins another coming in from the right from Ty Nant car park, go LEFT downhill for about 300 yards to reach the starting point.

Answer: Old War Department rifle range target holders.

WALK 10
GLYN ARAN

DESCRIPTION A moderate 4 mile walk which starts in Dolgellau but soon enters the wooded Glyn Aran, where there were once many fulling mills for the woollen industry. Later, in open countryside, there are fine views over Dolgellau and of the surrounding hills. Allow 3 hours.

START From the Leisure Centre car park in Dolgellau. SH 731178.

DIRECTIONS From the town centre stay on the south side of the Afon Wnion and take the road east towards the A470 to Machynlleth. Before leaving the built up area turn LEFT along the road between the Government office building and the bus depot, going past the fire station to the Leisure Centre.

1 Leave the car park through the entrance and immediately turn RIGHT into the supermarket car park. Go through it and then RIGHT to the road bridge over the Afon Aran. DO NOT cross the bridge, but cross the main road and continue alongside the river, passing in front of an attractive terrace of stone cottages. Carry on up to the end of the road and take the narrow road ahead uphill and half-RIGHT. Go up this road, passing a modern bungalow on the right, beyond which the surfacing ends. Continue along the unsurfaced track until a road is reached, close to the residence *Frongoch.*

2 At the road go RIGHT and walk along it. *This is uphill walking, but the slower pace means greater enjoyment of this lovely wooded valley, with the Afon Aran down below on the right.* After about ⅓ mile a road (the first) joins from the left, with a gate across it, signed *Tyddyn Ednyfed and Dref Gerig.* Turn LEFT through this gate and walk along the road. After about 200 yards, at a junction, continue straight ahead up to another gate at the edge of an evergreen wood. Go through this gate and continue ahead, but, after about 60 yards turn very sharp RIGHT along a signed footpath. Keep along the obvious path ahead, crossing a small stream and going through a gap in a substantial stone wall to reach the ruins of a former farmhouse on the left. Continue along the path, crossing two more small streams and then emerging out of the wood at a surfaced road alongside an old (1882) schoolhouse now converted into a dwelling.

3 Turn LEFT along the road, but go almost immediately RIGHT through a gate signed *Pandy Gader.* Go ahead across the field in front of the dwelling to cross a footbridge over the Afon Aran. Turn RIGHT along a roughly surfaced walled track. *Ignore the signed footpath to the left after about 60 yards,* and continue down the rough track. About 100 yards after this first footpath sign, the track goes through a gap in a wall. Turn LEFT immediately after this gap and cross a stile over a fence and into a wood. Go ahead, keeping fairly close to the wall on the left. When an area of moss-covered stones is reached, turn RIGHT and walk roughly parallel to another wall on the left and along a narrow path through more mossy boulders. The path reaches the low remains of an old wall and a waymark sign on a tree. Go ahead as indicated by the sign, soon going partly right and parallel to another wall ahead. Keep the wall on the left, and after about 75 yards the path reaches some more low remains of an old wall. Go through the gap and then half-LEFT to the waymark on a tree ahead (NOT straight ahead along the more obvious path). Carry on down to cross double stiles over a fence and a wall, to join a rough surfaced wide track. Turn RIGHT along it to reach a surfaced road.

4 Go LEFT along the road, passing *Parc Cottage* on the right. *This cottage was the home of the last person to be hanged in Dolgellau, Cadwaladr Jones, who confessed in 1877 to the murder of a young local woman.* Carry on along the road and, after going through a gate, passing the next house on the right, *Esgeiriau. The track opposite this property leads to Bryn Mawr, which was the home of Rowland Ellis, who became a prominent Quaker in the 17th century, and* *who led emigrants to the USA to escape persecution. He named his new settlement in Pennsylvania, Bryn Mawr, and the name was later given to the well-known women's college there.* Carry on along the road as it drops down to reach its lowest level, crossing the stream Nant y Ceunant.

5 When you reach the bridge go RIGHT through a gate along a signed wide track, with the stream below on the right. Keep along this wide green track as it moves away from the stream and rises slightly. *There are good views to the right of Mynydd Moel and soon, ahead, to Dolgellau and beyond.* When a wall ahead is approached, go RIGHT downhill, parallel to it, to reach a gate in the corner of the field. Go through the gate and along an old fenced track lined with some fine beech trees. *As the track drops down you will see how Dolgellau developed at a good crossing point of the Afon Wnion. The town's central older buildings, built of the dark grey volcanic stone and roofed with local slate, seem to fit more easily into the natural landscape than some of the later developments.*

6 Continue down to the first of the houses, and then go RIGHT and steeply downhill along another rough surfaced track. When a surfaced road is reached keep ahead, again steeply downhill, until an open area of crossroads is reached. Go ahead and slightly left and continue down to arrive at the town centre, Eldon Square.

To learn more about the Meirionnydd Quakers, the Information Centre in Eldon Square has both a leaflet published by the Snowdonia National Park and an extensive and very informative exhibition upstairs.

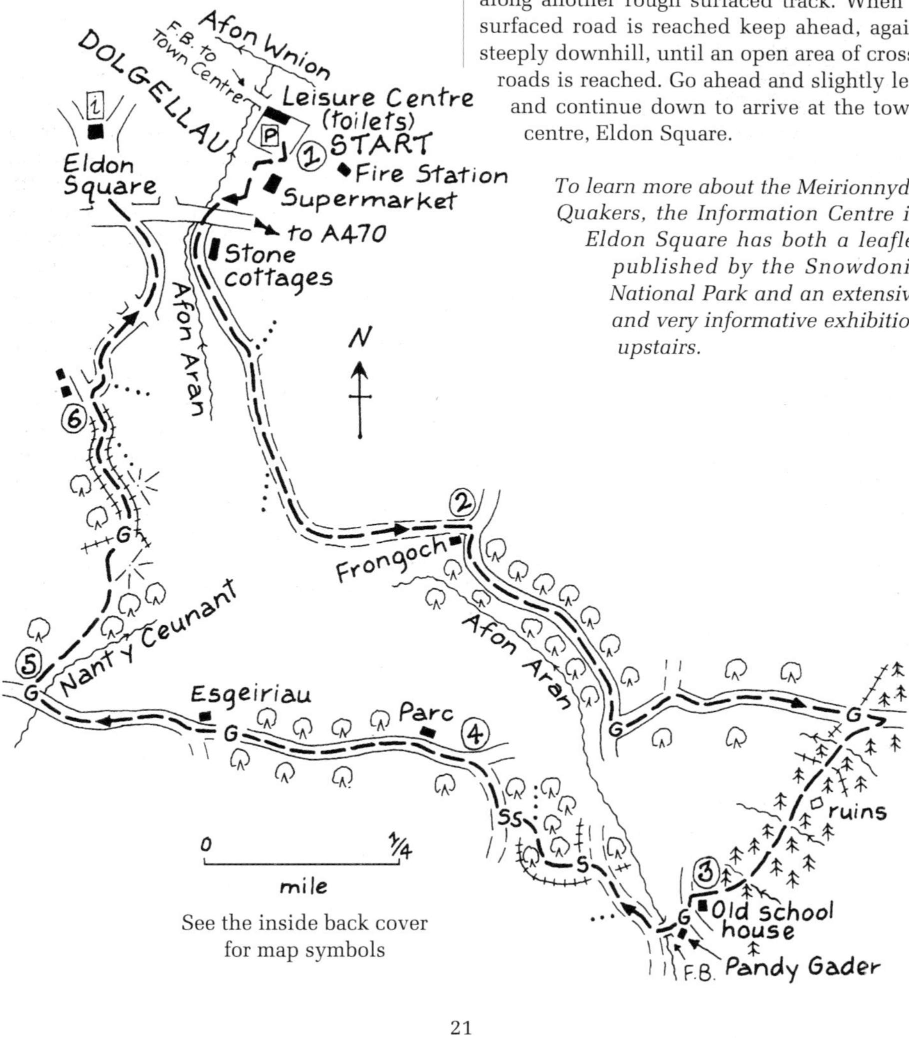

See the inside back cover for map symbols

WALK 11
TORRENT WALK

DESCRIPTION A popular and easy 2½ mile walk using a path close to a tumbling river in a beautiful ravine, and including the chance to visit the remains of an old charcoal blast furnace, used for smelting iron. This walk, enjoyable at all times, is at its very best after rain, when the river will be running full. Allow 1½ hours.

START Lay-by on the B4416 just west of Brithdir. SH 761181.

DIRECTIONS Take the A470 east from Dolgellau towards Machynlleth. After about 2 miles turn LEFT (east) along the B4416 towards Brithdir. After crossing the narrow bridge over the river, park in the first lay-by on the left side, a distance of ½ mile from the main A470 road.

The Torrent Walk was designed and engineered by Thomas Payne, who also designed the embankment across the estuary at Porthmadog, known as the Cob. There were originally walks on both sides of the ravine, and although planned as an extension of the gardens of Caerynwch house nearby, they were open to the public from their completion early in the 19th century. Thomas Payne died in Dolgellau in 1834 aged 73, and there is a memorial plate to him there in St Mary's church.

1 Walk along the road towards Brithdir. After 250 yards, opposite the entrance to St Mark's church, turn LEFT down a narrow minor road. *This partly tree-lined road is parallel to but well above the river, which is below you on your left, and which at times you will be able to hear but not see. This is a chance to enjoy the many varieties and different ages of the trees along the road, some of which seem to be growing out of the massive boulders at the base of their trunks. Part of this road is thought to be the line of an old Roman road leading to, and beyond, a Roman fortlet at Brithdir about 1 mile to the east.* After about ¾ mile, all downhill, the road joins another coming from the right.

2 Continue along to the LEFT past a group of cottages in an attractive valley-bottom setting. *These cottages were formerly a woollen mill and its associated warehouses.* After crossing the road bridge over the river – and having the first sight of the Afon Clywedog – the way into the Torrent Walk is through a gate immediately on your LEFT. However, by walking just a further 200 yards along the road and turning RIGHT into the drive of the Fronalchen caravan site, it is possible to view the remains of an early 18th century charcoal blast furnace. *These remains, a little way down the entrance drive on the right hand side, were excavated and consolidated in 1982 and 1983 by students from the Snowdonia National Park Study Centre at Maentwrog. A detailed pamphlet about this, the Dolgun Blast Furnace, is available from the Park's offices.*

3 Return to the bridge and turn RIGHT into the Torrent Walk. For some way ahead the path remains on about the same level as the river but it gradually climbs, eventually leaving the river well below. However, the ascent is never steep, and there are short flights of steps in places to assist the climb. *The beauty of the gorge, and the continually varying views of the Clywedog tumbling over and around the rocks and boulders in its path, make this a walk to be taken slowly. There is a seat, about two thirds of the way up the path, provided by the North Wales Wildlife Trust in memory of Mary Richards, a well known local botanist who died in 1977.*

4 At the top of the ravine cross the footbridge over the river *(constructed about 1970 to replace Thomas Payne's original crossing)* and go out through the swing-gate ahead to the road. Turn LEFT along the road to return to the lay-by just 100 yards ahead.

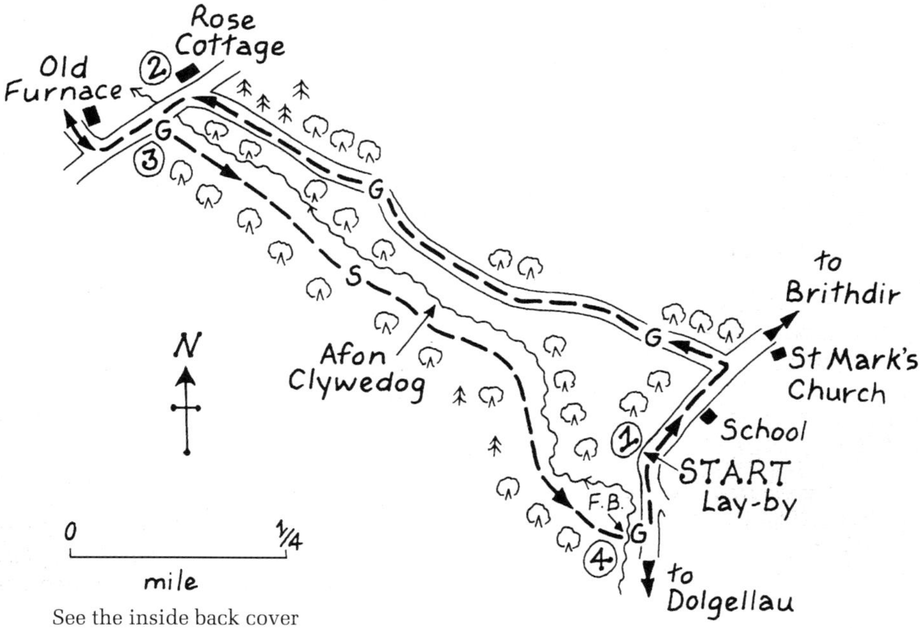

See the inside back cover for map symbols

After the walk, try to make time for a visit to the nearby St Mark's Church. It is formally listed as a building of special architectural and historic interest, and one of the very few such buildings in Wales to be classed as Grade 1. It was the major work of Henry Wilson, one of the leading post-William Morris figures of the Arts & Crafts Movement. The interior is richly painted and contains some remarkable high quality copper furnishings. Many architectural historians consider it an important and advanced work for its time of completion, in 1898.

St Mark's Church, Brithdir

WALK 12
LLYNNAU CREGENNEN

DESCRIPTION A mainly level 5½ mile walk in an area many people consider to be the most beautiful in Meirionnydd. There are fine views of the dominating northern escarpment of Cadair Idris for much of the walk, which also includes a superb riverside path in the wooded Afon Gwynant valley. Allow 3 hours.

START Car park at Cregennen Lakes. SH 658142.

DIRECTIONS Leave Dolgellau from the top (southern) end of Eldon Square along the road to Tywyn. After about ½ mile take the minor road half-LEFT signed 'Cadair Idris'. Go about 4½ miles and then take the road signed 'Cregennen Lakes' to the RIGHT. The car park is ¾ mile along this road, on the left.

1 Leave the car park and go LEFT along the road for about 300 yards to reach a low waymark post. *Look left here for a view down to the Mawddach Estuary. The land across the horizon is the Llyn Peninsula.* Go sharp RIGHT across open ground to a ladder stile over a wall.

2 Cross the stile and take the path half-RIGHT through the heather. (*The path half-left takes you to the top of the steep hill – Pared y Cefn-hir – if you are feeling energetic. There are fine views from the top and it is possible to walk along the ridge and drop down at the end to rejoin the walk near point 3 at Ty'n Llidiart).* Continue along the path (ignoring the waymark sign to the right soon after passing the lake) and reach a high, but partly broken, stone wall on the right. The path continues roughly parallel to the wall. After a while it goes slightly uphill, over a brief boggy area, and then soon drops down close to the wall. *There are views to your right to the Craig-las escarpment, at about 2200 feet.* Soon the path curves left and runs alongside a wall at right angles to the one followed so far. Continue along the path as it drops down and turns RIGHT downhill to a gate in the wall ahead.

3 Go through the gate and then half-RIGHT across a field to another gate in a wall, about 50 yards ahead. Continue through this gate and go half-LEFT to reach a gap in the wall 100 yards ahead. Go through and carry on parallel, and soon close, to a low wall on the right. The path becomes a farm vehicle track. Keep along it and, where it divides, keep RIGHT towards a small group of trees, and then on to a gate ahead. Go through the gate and keep on the track, until a surfaced road is reached. Go LEFT along the road for about 200 yards, with the stream dropping lower into a ravine on the right, to a ruined chapel on the left, *where the cemetery is still used.*

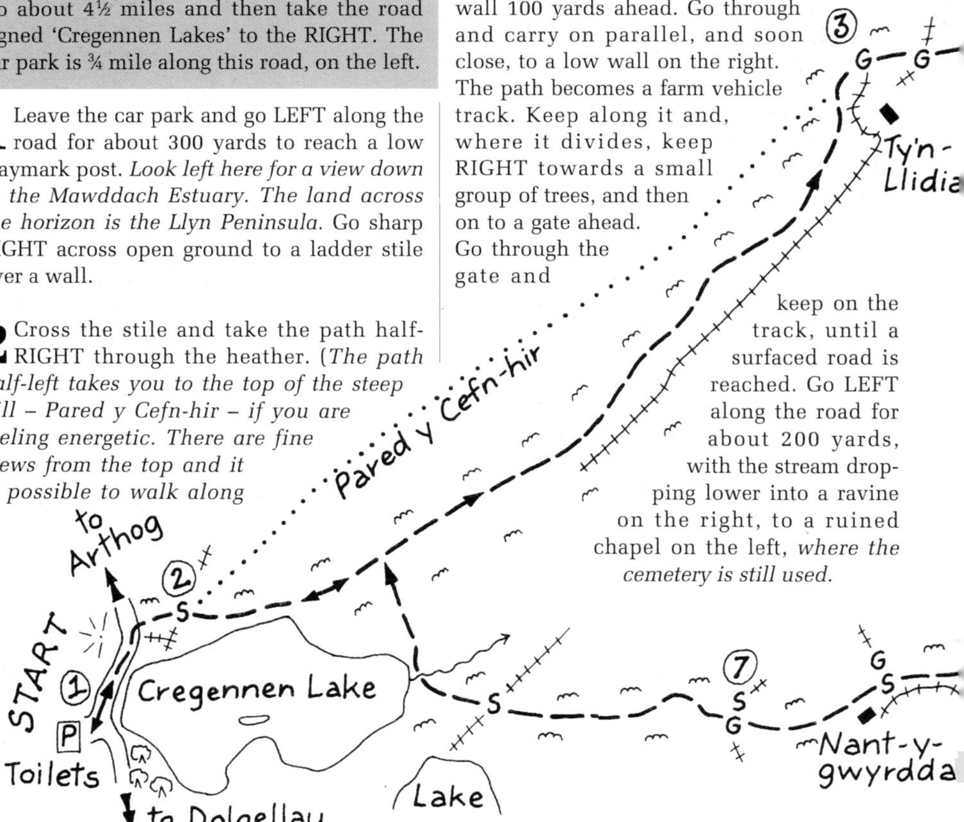

4 At the cemetery gates go RIGHT along a wide path into a wood and follow this down until a gate is reached. Go through and up to a surfaced road. Turn RIGHT downhill, and in 100 yards, at a road junction, turn RIGHT again and pass in front of a youth hostel. Cross the river at the road bridge and then immediately go RIGHT through a gate into a field with the river on your right.

5 Go across the field to a gate ahead. Pass through it and continue along the path through trees. After a while the path climbs slightly and curves LEFT alongside a fence to reach a swing gate. Go through and turn RIGHT to reach a sloping field. Keep straight ahead across the bottom of the field to a narrow stone footbridge, surmounted by a small gate, across two streams. Pass through into another field and carry on ahead with a low wall on the right. *The river is below to the right and there are soon views of Cadair Idris ahead.* Keep along this path. It gradually drops down close to the river and becomes a rough surfaced track. Another, but more substantial, footbridge is reached. Cross it and go ahead uphill along the rough track and through a gate at the top. *The farm down on the right serves teas.* Cross the track leading to the farm and carry on straight ahead along the rough open track across the field to a gate in the far corner, close to farm buildings.

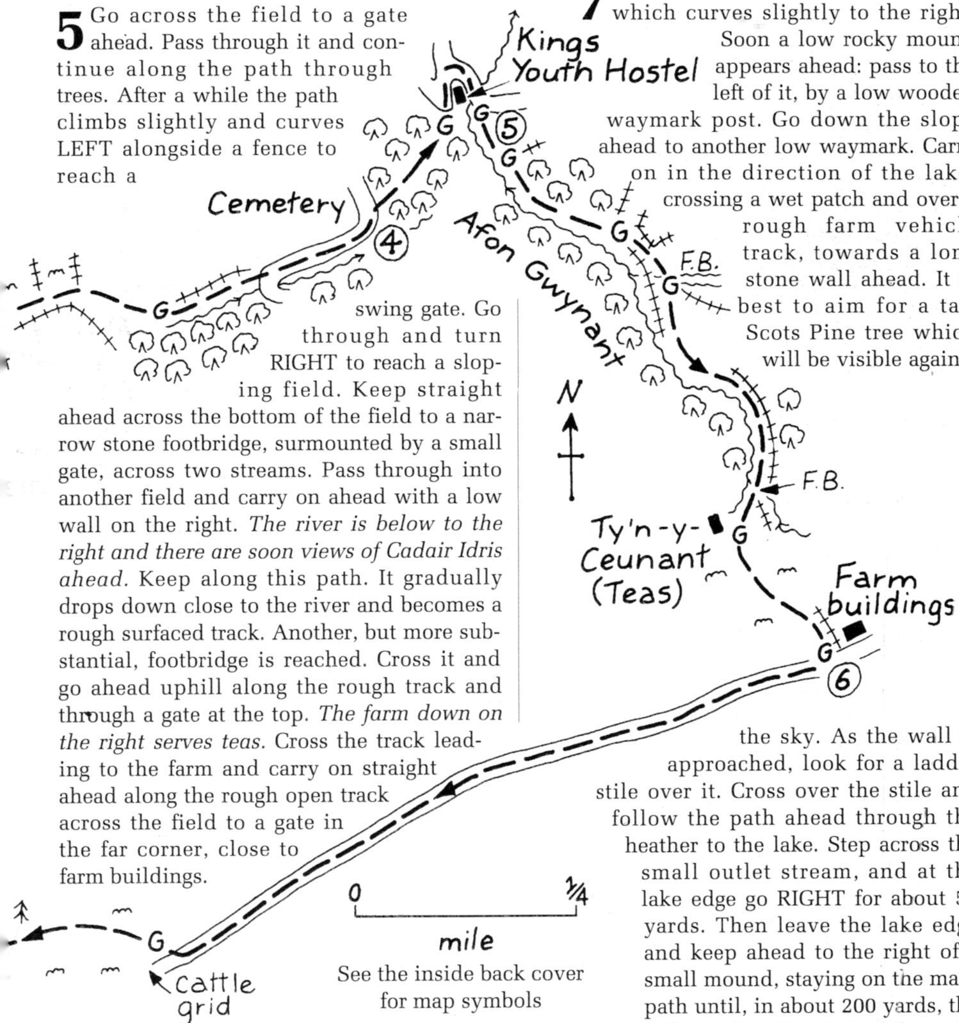

See the inside back cover for map symbols

6 Go through the gate and turn RIGHT along a minor unclassified road. Stay on this road for about ¾ mile and, just before a cattle grid, turn off RIGHT along a rough surfaced track signed *Nantygwyrddail Farm.* Continue along it to the farm. Pass to the right of the outbuildings and cross a ladder stile alongside a gate in the wall ahead. Carry on along the slightly uphill track to reach another ladder stile. Cross this. The larger Cregennen Lake comes into view.

7 Continue ahead along the track, which curves slightly to the right. Soon a low rocky mound appears ahead: pass to the left of it, by a low wooden waymark post. Go down the slope ahead to another low waymark. Carry on in the direction of the lake, crossing a wet patch and over a rough farm vehicle track, towards a long stone wall ahead. It is best to aim for a tall Scots Pine tree which will be visible against the sky. As the wall is approached, look for a ladder stile over it. Cross over the stile and follow the path ahead through the heather to the lake. Step across the small outlet stream, and at the lake edge go RIGHT for about 50 yards. Then leave the lake edge and keep ahead to the right of a small mound, staying on the main path until, in about 200 yards, the path used at the start of the walk is reached. Turn LEFT along it to return to the car park.

WALK 13
LLYN GWERNAN AND AN OLD TRACKWAY

DESCRIPTION A 4 mile moderate walk in beautiful, undulating mixed scenery. Initially there are fine views of the northern escarpment of Cadair Idris and of the hills across the wooded Gwynant valley, followed by very extensive views to the far hills and mountains north and east of Dolgellau. The route partly traces an old trackway and passes close to prehistoric burial cairns and hill forts. The final section is alongside Llyn Gwernan. Allow 2 – 2½ hours.

START Snowdonia National Park car park and picnic area at Ty Nant, 3 miles south west of Dolgellau. SH 698152.

DIRECTIONS Leave Dolgellau town centre from the top (southern) end of Eldon Square along the road towards Tywyn. After about ½ mile go half-LEFT along the minor road signed Cadair Idris. The car park is 3 miles further along, on the right.

1 Leave the car park by going out on to the farm lane passing close to the right of the toilets. Turn LEFT along it, go through a gate and continue ahead along the track signed *Tyddyn Farm*. After about 100 yards, where the track divides, keep straight ahead and go through a gate. Continue along the track through two more gates to reach the farm. Keeping close to a wall on the left, go through another gate to pass close to the left of the farm buildings. Leave the farmyard area by going ahead through yet another gate and on to a grass covered track, with a fence on the left. Carry on through a gate ahead, continuing along the track. After about 50 yards go slightly RIGHT through a gap in the wall, but continue in the same general direction, now with a fence on the right and a wall on the left.

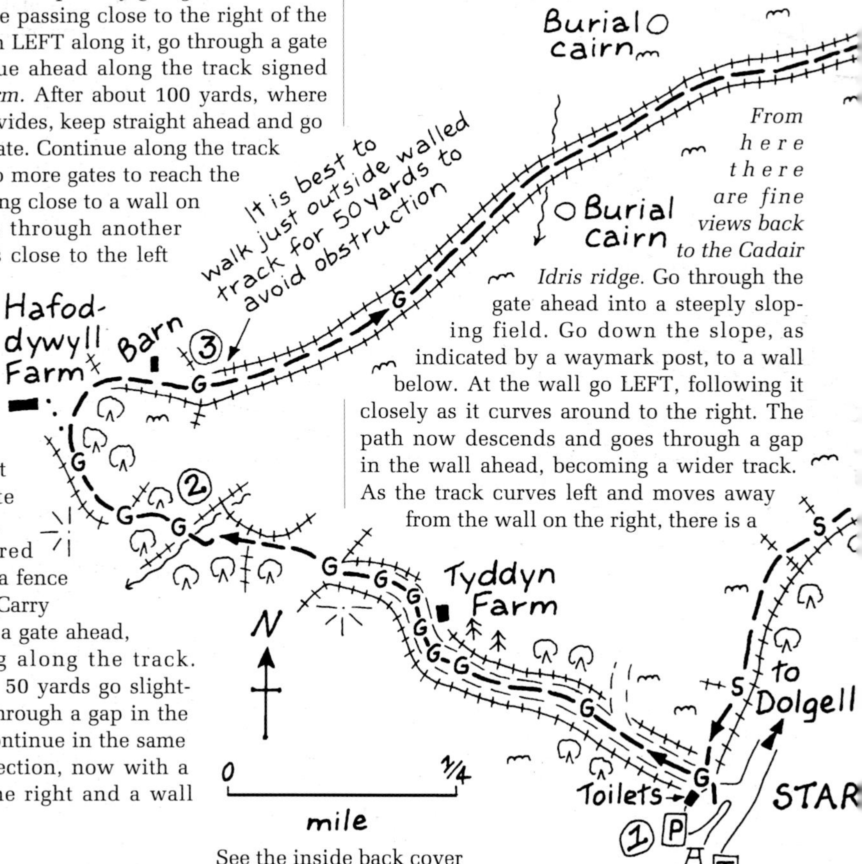

From here there are fine views back to the Cadair Idris ridge. Go through the gate ahead into a steeply sloping field. Go down the slope, as indicated by a waymark post, to a wall below. At the wall go LEFT, following it closely as it curves around to the right. The path now descends and goes through a gap in the wall ahead, becoming a wider track. As the track curves left and moves away from the wall on the right, there is a

See the inside back cover for map symbols

yellow waymark on an oak tree to the left of the track. Just 20 yards past this tree go RIGHT down the grassy slope to reach a stream and a wall.

2 Cross the stream near the gate in the wall, and go through the gate and up to a farm vehicle track 10 yards ahead. Go LEFT along the track for 10 yards and then half-RIGHT along a narrow path amongst the birch and oak trees. One of the trees has a waymark. Follow this path to a gate in the fence. Go through the gate and turn LEFT, keeping close to the fence. The path becomes a track and soon goes through a gate and on to a

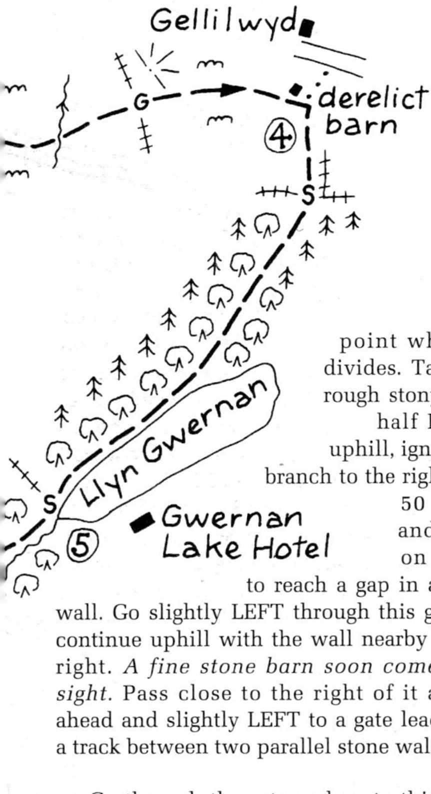

point where it divides. Take the rough stony track half RIGHT uphill, ignoring a branch to the right after 50 yards, and carry on ahead to reach a gap in a stone wall. Go slightly LEFT through this gap but continue uphill with the wall nearby on the right. *A fine stone barn soon comes into sight.* Pass close to the right of it and go ahead and slightly LEFT to a gate leading to a track between two parallel stone walls.

3 Go through the gate and on to this track. Because of a blockage not far ahead it is better for the next 50 yards to walk just outside this walled track, on the left-hand side, but then dropping down on to it just past the short stone wall built across the track. Now keep along this walled track for the whole of its length of just over 1 mile. *The origins of this old track are not clear, but it could be prehistoric, as there are a number of burial cairns close to it, as well as two Iron Age hill forts. The parallel walls suggest later use as a drove route for local hill farmers.* After walking the track for a little over ¼ mile a gate is reached. *From here the remains of a hill fort can be seen on the ridge across the valley on the right – not at the highest point but at a rocky mound about half-way down. It is named Craig y Castell on OS maps. Look also for the burial cairns shown on the map.* The end of this walled track is at a gate in a wall. Go through it and carry on ahead along a wide grass track, passing to the right of a high gorse-covered mound. Cross a small stream and continue down the track as it curves left and then right to reach a gate in a fence. Go through the gate and follow the track down to a derelict farm building.

4 Turn RIGHT here along a rough stone track, soon with a fence on the left, to reach a ladder stile. Cross the stile and go half-RIGHT along the narrow path into the wooded area. Continue ahead through the trees. Follow the path to the lake edge and keep along it to the right, reaching a ladder stile over a wall, at the end of the lake.

5 Cross over this stile and walk along the narrow path through trees, keeping to the right of the lake's outlet stream. Stay on this path, going through a gap in a wall and continuing along its winding way to reach a ladder stile over a wall. Go over and ahead to another ladder stile. Cross it and continue along the path in an open area keeping roughly parallel to the wall on the left. As a wall ahead is approached go half-RIGHT to pass through a gap into the next open area. There is then a low waymarked post just 15 yards ahead. Follow the half-LEFT direction indicated, aiming for the far end of the stone wall over to the left. Two low yellow-topped posts near the end of the wall indicate the path, which carries on to another (the last!) ladder stile, partly hidden in the field corner ahead. Cross this stile and proceed away from, but roughly parallel to, the wall on the left to return to the car park.

WALK 14
LLYN Y GADAIR

DESCRIPTION A moderately energetic 4½ mile walk, mainly in open country. On the outward part, the towering cliffs of the Cadair Idris northern escarpment get closer and closer until the route reaches the lovely Llyn y Gadair, set below Cadair's high peaks. The uphill walk to the lake has some fairly steep sections, and the ¾ mile immediately before reaching the lake crosses open moorland. *This section must not be undertaken in mist or very low cloud. After heavy rain, the outlet stream from Llyn y Gadair can be difficult to cross – search for the easiest point.* The return from the lake is along the lower section of the well used *Foxes Path* and is all downhill, with fine views across the Mawddach valley. If visibility is good this is an exceptional walk for all who enjoy dramatic views. Allow 3 to 4 hours.

START National Park car park and picnic area at Ty Nant. SH 698152.

DIRECTIONS Leave Dolgellau from the top (southern) end of Eldon Square along Cadair Road towards Tywyn. After ½ mile, just before a petrol station, take the minor road half-LEFT signed Cadair Idris. The car park is 3 miles further along, on the right.

1 From the car park go back out onto the road and turn RIGHT along it. After about 150 yards, at a telephone booth, go LEFT along a wide rough surfaced track leading to *Ty Nant*. Carry on past the farm buildings through a swing gate ahead alongside a stream and over a footbridge. Keep on ahead along the track with a stream on the right and, later, another on the left. When a slightly more open area is reached, follow the waymark direction around to the RIGHT to go between two stone walls. Go through a swing gate – *there is a memorial tablet here* – and cross the footbridge to continue along the path with a fence on the right. An open area with a waymark post is soon reached. Go LEFT uphill as directed. The path becomes stepped in places and, after about ¼ mile, reaches a gate in a wall.

2 Go through the gate and continue along the wide, green path ahead for about ¼ mile to reach another gate in a wall. Go through it and immediately cross a bridge over a small stream. Pass a ladder stile in the wall on the right, and walk on to another bridge over a small stream just 40 yards beyond the ladder stile. *DO NOT* cross this bridge but go very sharp LEFT onto a grassy mound. Look for a narrow path up ahead about 12 yards from the small stream on the right, running roughly parallel to it. It goes in a south-easterly direction towards the highest point of Cyfrwy ahead. *It is important to locate this narrow track* because there are few landmarks hereabouts, but once on the track it can be followed right across this area. After about 100 yards the track curves slightly LEFT away from the stream. Keep along it, all the time going towards the near-vertical high rock escarpment and screes ahead. Cross a small stream, and when some large grassy mounds are reached the track goes slightly LEFT to avoid them. It passes about 30 yards to the right of the ruins of a shepherd's cottage. Here, carry on ahead on the track as it goes to the LEFT of the low shoulder of a grass covered mound.

3 The track soon passes about 30 yards to the left of an old sheep pen, and the rock and screes at the base of Cyfrwy become fully visible. The aim now is to reach the grass covered mounds ahead, immediately to the left of the rock covered area. When the path reaches an area completely covered with rocks go slightly LEFT across them and out to the track, now again through heather. At the base of the next grassy mound follow the track as it curves RIGHT and up to the top of the mound. It goes along the ridge at the top of the mound with a mass of tangled boulders down on the right. When the ridge drops slightly, and about 30 yards before rocks covering the ridge ahead, go LEFT down and then up a grassy ridge to the left of a large hollowed out area. Carry on along the path on this ridge and when at the head of the gully on the right, follow the path slightly RIGHT as it rises up the grassy slope ahead. Look for a vertical, small, but distinctive rock at the very top of the mound ahead, appearing like an isolated miniature standing stone. Follow the path towards it. *At this rock, part of Llyn y Gadair is now visible ahead.* Carry on along the path towards the lake, down and up amongst the rocks. There are choices, but keep aiming towards the lake and it will soon be reached. *It has a wonderful setting below Penygadair (2928 ft), the highest point of the Cadair Idris range.*

4 When you decide to leave, go LEFT along the lake edge to the point furthest away from the crags, where the path goes down through boulders alongside the small gully made by the lake's outlet stream. Carry on down the main path. The path passes close to the left of another lake, Llyn Gafr.

Cross the outlet stream and carry on along the broad path ahead. It crosses a flat area then curves left to another stream. Cross this and go immediately LEFT along its bank. After about 100 yards a wall is reached. Go through the gap in it and turn sharp LEFT to follow the narrow path alongside the wall and stream. In another 100 yards, just before a fence, the path goes to the RIGHT and then becomes a broad green track. Carry on along this, roughly parallel to the fence on the left. Cross a small stream close to the fence and keep walking down to reach a swing gate in a wall.

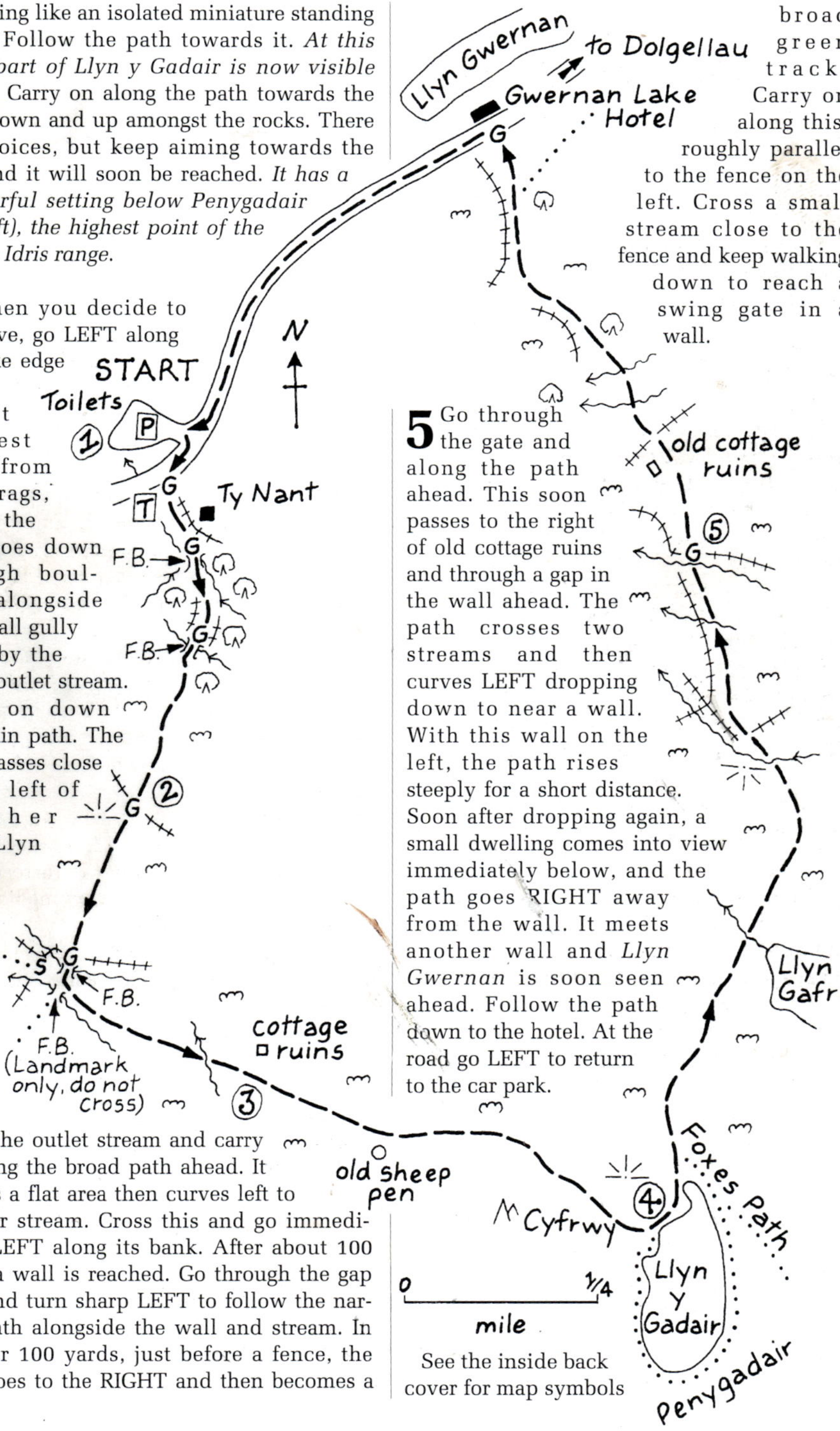

5 Go through the gate and along the path ahead. This soon passes to the right of old cottage ruins and through a gap in the wall ahead. The path crosses two streams and then curves LEFT dropping down to near a wall. With this wall on the left, the path rises steeply for a short distance. Soon after dropping again, a small dwelling comes into view immediately below, and the path goes RIGHT away from the wall. It meets another wall and *Llyn Gwernan* is soon seen ahead. Follow the path down to the hotel. At the road go LEFT to return to the car park.

See the inside back cover for map symbols

1 Leave the car park by the swing gate close to the toilets and turn RIGHT along the wide rough surfaced track. Follow this track to reach another swing gate. Go through it and turn LEFT. After crossing a bridge over a small river go RIGHT, and through a gate into a wooded area. Follow the stepped track up, and through another gate, into open countryside. Continue along the clear track, soon with a mountain stream close on the right.

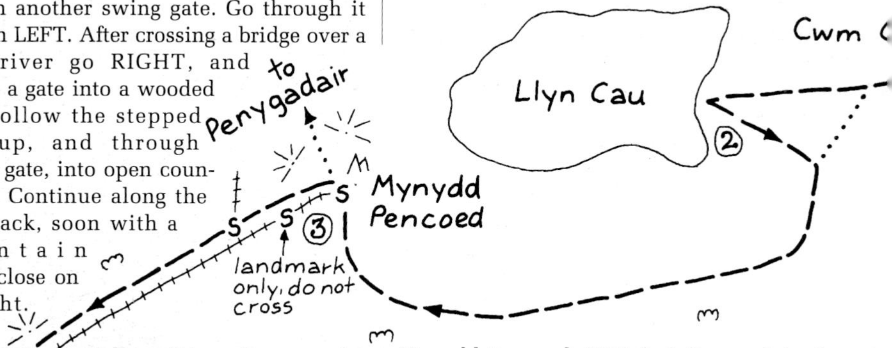

Follow this path upwards, generally now less steeply, as it curves left and then right into the upper valley of Cwm Cau. As the path ascends to the rim ahead, keep straight ahead, ignoring paths to the left, into the basin to reach the lake, Llyn Cau. *It is at a height of about 1500 feet, is about 130 feet deep and set in a fine example of a glaciated basin. This wild area is home to upland birds such as the raven and ring ouzel. The pyramid top straight ahead is the summit of Mynydd Pencoed, 2617 feet. Penygadair, the summit of Cadair Idris, is just out of sight to the right.*

2 To continue the walk, turn around from the lake and look back along the route taken to reach it. Then go half-RIGHT across the grassy area to reach the stony track going steeply up to the ridge on the right. Go up this track to the top. Turn RIGHT and follow the well worn track around this southern ridge high above Llyn Cau, eventually crossing a ladder stile to stand on the top of Mynydd Pencoed. *This is a dramatic viewpoint, encompassing Penygadair, 2928 feet, about ¾ mile to the north. The route to it is obvious and clear for those who wish to take it, and if you have the time and energy it is a pity to miss going to the summit.*

3 This walk continues from the summit of Mynydd Pencoed along the broad ridge away from Llyn Cau. Follow the fence south-westwards, keeping it on your left. Ignore the

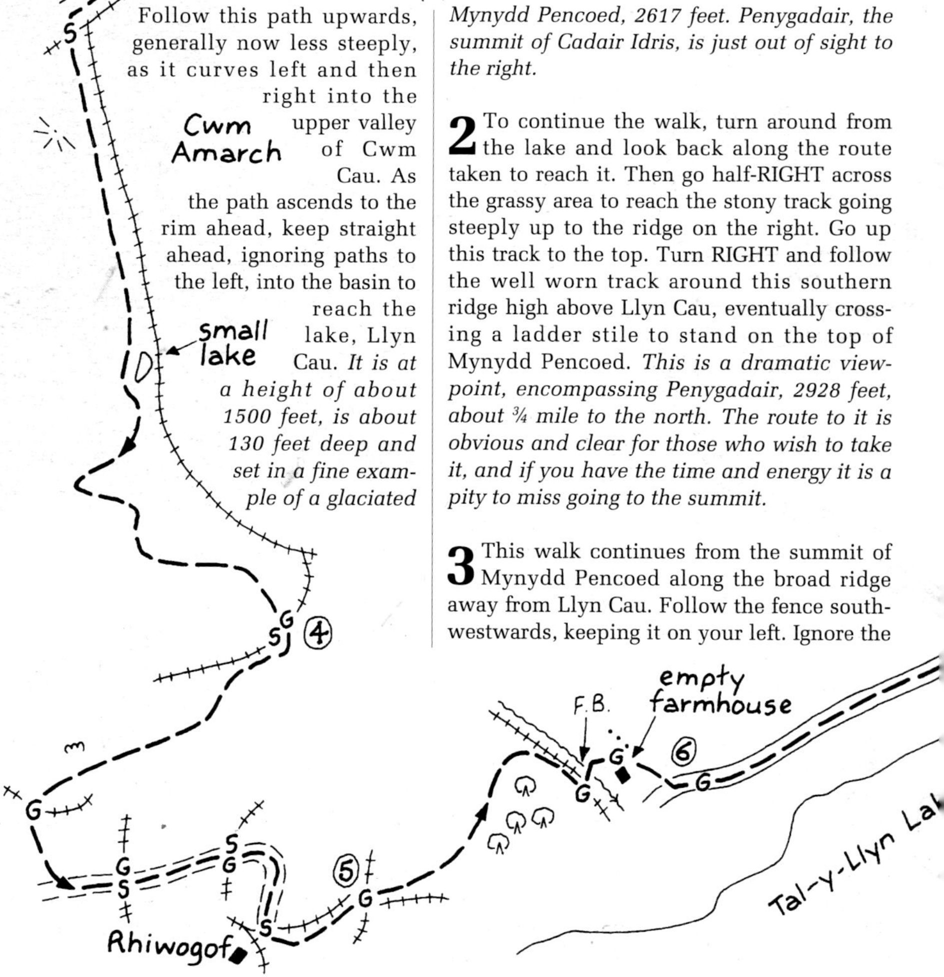

WALK 15
LLYN CAU, CADAIR IDRIS & TAL-Y-LLYN

DESCRIPTION A challenging and fairly strenuous 7 mile walk. It first reaches Llyn Cau, a spectacular glacial lake, closely enclosed on three sides by towering rock and scree, and then climbs above the lake to the summit of Mynydd Pencoed (2617 feet) for extensive views in all directions. From here the summit of Cadair Idris itself (2928 feet) can easily be reached. The return is by a little used but easy route around the top of another cwm, to drop down to the side of the Tal-y-llyn lake. *This is the most challenging walk in this book, and should not be attempted in bad weather.* On a fine, clear, day it is very rewarding. Allow 5½ hours, but 7 hours if extending the walk to include the summit of Cadair Idris.

START The Dol Idris Snowdonia National Park car park at Minffordd. SH 732115.

DIRECTIONS Leave Dolgellau on the A470 towards Machynlleth, turning RIGHT along the A487 at the Cross Foxes Inn, 3 miles out of the town. After a further 4 miles turn RIGHT along the B4405, signed Tywyn, and almost immediately turn RIGHT again into the car park.

ladder stile in the fence after about 100 yards, and carry on to reach a low fence directly ahead, across the route being taken. Cross it by the stile and continue ahead, still keeping parallel to the fence on the left. After about ¼ mile another ladder stile is reached in this fence. Cross the stile and go down alongside the fence on the left. Go down to the small lake ahead and pass to the right of it, close to the outlying pools, and follow the faint track of the farmer's mountain vehicle. These tracks move closer to the fence after rounding the knoll behind the lake, but when the land is about to drop very steeply they turn right to take a less steep zig-zag route down. This is preferable to following the fence closely. Whichever route is taken, the aim is to reach the fence and wall at the bottom of the slope, running at right angles to the fence on the left.

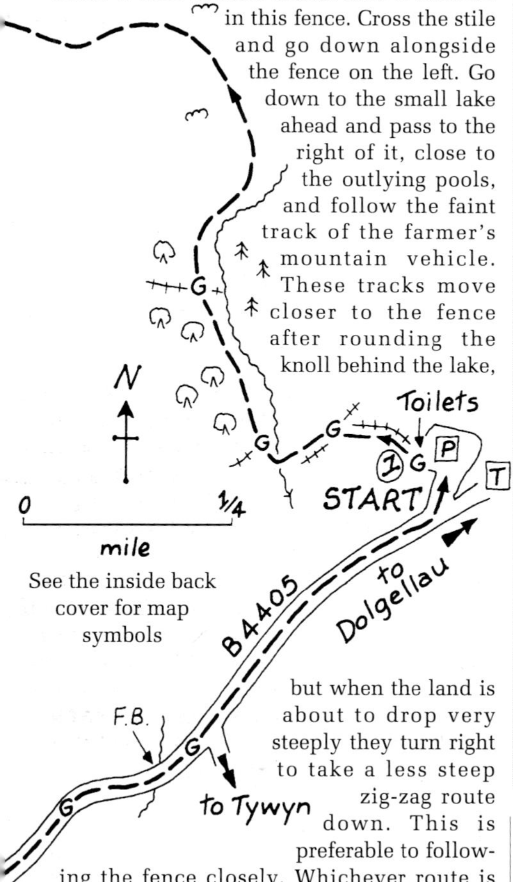

See the inside back cover for map symbols

4 Go through the gate in the fence ahead and a gap in the wall, and follow the vehicle tracks to the right, staying on them as they take an easy route down to the next gate. Go through it and then half-LEFT down to join the rough surfaced road. Turn LEFT and keep on the road, crossing two stiles, to the farm *Rhiwogof* below. At the farm approach, cross the stile in the fence ahead and go LEFT alongside the fence.

5 Go through the gate ahead and continue along the track, which soon drops down into the steep-sided valley containing the stream flowing swiftly out of Cwm Amarch. Turn RIGHT along the fence above the stream and then, near the bottom of the field, go LEFT through a gate. Cross the stream by the footbridge and go through the gate ahead. Follow the track down to the surfaced road.

6 Turn LEFT and follow this farm access road which, after 3 gates and a footbridge alongside a ford, joins the B4405 road to return to the car park ahead.

WELSH

The meanings of some of the common words found in local place names

aber	mouth
afon	river, stream
allt	hillside
bach	small
banc	hill
blaen	head of valley
bont	bridge
bryn	hill
bwlch	pass
cadair (cader)	chair
caer	fort
capel	chapel
castell	castle
cefn	ridge
ceunant	ravine
coch	red
coed	wood
craig	rock
croes	cross
cwm	valley
dinas	fort, city
dol	meadow
du	black
dwr	water
dyffryn	valley
eglwys	church
esgair	hillspur
fach	small
fan	high place
fawr	large
fechan	small
felin	mill
ffordd	road
ffynnon	spring, well
foel	bare hill
fynydd	mountain
garth	enclosure, hill
glas	green, blue
glyder	heap
glyn	glen
gors	bog
grug	heather
gwen	white
gyrn	peak
hafod	summer dwelling
hen	old
hendre	winter dwelling
heol	road
hir	long
isaf	lowest
llan	church
llech	slate
llidiart	gate
llwyd	grey
llyn	lake
maen	stone
maes	field
mawr	big
melin	mill
moch	pigs
moel	bare hill
mor	sea
mynach	monk
mynydd	mountain
nant	stream
neuadd	hall
newydd	new
ogof	cave
pandy	mill
pant	hollow
parc	field, park
pen	top
penmaen	rocky headland
pistyll	waterfall, spout
plas	mansion
porth	port
pwll	pool
rhaeadr	waterfall
rhiw	hill
rhos	marsh, moor
rhyd	ford
sarn	road
sych	dry
tarren	hill
tomen	mound
traeth	shore, beach
traws	across
tref	hamlet, home
twll	hole
ty	house
uchaf	highest
y, yr	the, of the
ynys	island
ysgol	school
ystrad	valley floor